Mystical Meditations

on the

Collects

Mystical
Meditations
on the
Collects

———*by*———

DION FORTUNE

SAMUEL WEISER, INC.
York Beach, Maine

First American paperback published in 1991 by
Samuel Weiser, Inc.
Box 612
York Beach, Maine 03910

Originally published in London in 1930 by
Rider & Co.

Library of Congress Cataloging–in–Publication Data

Fortune, Dion
      Mystical meditations on the collects / Dion Fortune.
         p.   cm.
      Reprint. Originally published: London : Rider, 1930.
        1. Collects—Meditations. 2. Church of England—Prayer–books and
devotions—English. 3. Anglican Communion—Prayer–books and
devotions—English. 4. Church year meditations. I. Title.
      BX5145.A62F66 1991
      242—dc20   91–12148
                                                       CIP
ISBN 0-87728-734-1
BJ

Cover painting is the "Garden of Eden," by Jan Brueghel the Elder (1568–1625),
oil on panel. Used by the courtesy of the Board of Trustees of the Victoria and
Albert Museum, London.

Printed in the United States of America

INTRODUCTION

IN offering these meditations on the collects to a wider public than that for which they were originally intended some explanation is necessary. The writer came to Christ by a winding way, and the stains of travel are upon her garments. The practice of the New Psychology, especially psycho-analysis, gave a certain understanding of human consciousness and supplied a vocabulary. The study of Theosophy, New Thought, Spiritualism, and other similar movements gave a new outlook on life.

From these different schools of thought she withdrew successively because of fundamental differences in outlook and certain camels that could not be swallowed, but which it is needless to specify here. Nevertheless, there were inestimable things for which she was indebted to these teachings, and they sent her back to the Christian Creed with an entirely new concept of its significance and a new understanding of the manner in which it could be approached.

The concept of an esoteric aspect to the great religions of the East set her seeking a similar aspect in the religion of the West ; this she found, both in the writings of the great mystics of the Christian faith and in personal experience. The mystical Christianity of the saints is the esotericism of the Christian church. It is not for all, for but few can achieve the consciousness of the Inner Mansions ; nevertheless it is there, awaiting the discovery of those who desire a deeper teaching than the pulpits give to the public.

It will be seen in the following pages that the writer takes Our Lord Jesus Christ as the Great Initiator and the Way of the Cross as the Path, thus giving a Christian form to concepts so familiar in esoteric literature. The traditional teachings of the Church are considered from a new angle, and a new aspect is thus brought into view.

The message of these pages may be defined as an intellectual mysticism. It says to the intellect, There is a spiritual mode of consciousness which alone reveals spiritual facts ; learn to function with that consciousness, and you will experience these facts for yourself and see upon what foundations the Christian faith is built.

It says to the mystic, Your mode of expression is incomprehensible to the man who has no concept of consciousness save as sensation and reason. You must translate your teaching into words that have a meaning for him if you are to convey any significance to his mind and assuage the hunger of his heart.

> " How can I tell, and how can you receive it
> Until he bringeth you where I have been ? "

This was the cry of a great mystical soul, but it is also the cry of a baffled soul, one that is forced to admit its own inability to help its fellow-men, much as it loves them.

We must find some way of bridging the great gulf which is fixed between the ordinary man, and the kingdom of the Saints. The realisations of the mystic have little value for any one except himself unless he is able to express them in terms comprehensible to the intellect which has had no special experience.

These facts of the Inner Life must be brought home to men's business and bosoms if they are to lift the burden of mankind and enlighten those who sit in darkness. It is not to the converted only that we must preach, nor yet to sinners who reject salvation, but to those who have begun to hunger and thirst after spiritual things but cannot accept them in the form in which they are usually presented.

The presentation adopted in these pages may not only cause scandal to the orthodox, but also to the heterodox, who desire to escape from the old bondage and find new pastures of the soul. The writer believes that the Christian faith is capable of a presentation which shall lead the intellect on to spiritual realisations, and that such a presentation will be welcomed by thoughtful men and women who, while keenly aware of their need for a deeper interpretation of life, cannot accept supernatural dogmas in blind faith.

To these the writer offers this little book. Whatever else it may or may not be, it is at least the fruit of actual experience.

CONTENTS

SAINTS' DAYS

MYSTICAL MEDITATIONS
ON THE COLLECTS

THE FIRST SUNDAY IN ADVENT

" ALMIGHTY God, give us grace that we may cast away the works of darkness, and put upon us the armour of light, now in the time of this mortal life, in which thy Son Jesus Christ came to visit us in great humility ; that in the last day, when he shall come again in his glorious Majesty to judge both the quick and the dead, we may rise to the life immortal, through him who liveth and reigneth with thee and the Holy Ghost, now and ever. Amen."

KEYNOTE : PURIFICATION OF CHARACTER

The first week in Advent has for its keynote the purification of character. " Almighty God, give us grace that we may cast away the works of darkness, and put upon us the armour of light, now in the time of this mortal life," prays the collect.

Character is the only basis upon which the Temple of mystical consciousness can be built. Let us therefore take for our standard the Divine Life lived in Galilee and cast out from consciousness every thought that is incompatible with that Ideal. Supposing we were walking in the company of the Master, would we care to utter such a thought ? No. Then do not let us think it in our own company.

We know neither the day nor the hour when the Son of Man cometh. The Risen Christ, who is the Master of Mystics, comes to us whenever consciousness is exalted into realisation by a wave of emotion. But these waves of emotion are transient. A man who leaps up and grasps a bar above his head must immediately draw himself up onto his support if he is to be safe ; he cannot hang by his hands for long. So it is with a wave of religious emotion ; it enables us to leap up above our habitual level of life and grasp that which is normally out of our reach ; but unless we can draw ourselves up bodily to that level we cannot retain our grasp upon it, and will soon drop back again.

Unless we have purified and disciplined our natures we shall only be able to grasp the hem of the Seamless Robe with our hands when the Lord comes to us in the stillness of the Silence ; we may be raised to His feet for a moment by a wave of emotion, but we shall inevitably drop back again unless we can draw our whole nature up to the level of the Christ-consciousness. We must be Christ-like if we are to abide with Christ.

THE SECOND SUNDAY IN ADVENT

" BLESSED Lord, who hast caused all holy Scriptures to
be written for our learning ; grant that we may in such
wise hear them, read, mark, learn, and inwardly digest
them, that by patience, and comfort of thy holy Word,
we may embrace and ever hold fast the blessed hope of
everlasting life, which thou hast given us in our Saviour
Jesus Christ. Amen."

KEYNOTE : MYSTICAL CONSCIOUSNESS

People often think that religion is only for the simple-
minded, and that any one whose intellect demands satisfaction will go empty away. This is due to a misunderstanding and confusion in the use of terms, and to
the application to spiritual experiences of expressions
associated with intellectual processes.

We must " in such wise " read the Scriptures that we
shall understand them. There is a technique of consciousness to be employed in spiritual realisation. We
cannot apply to it the same methods that would enable
us to solve a philosophical problem. We cannot arrive
by reasoning at an understanding of spiritual things.
We perceive spiritual things, in the first place, by means
of our feelings ; these are our sense-organs upon the
higher planes. Our emotions react to a spiritual stimulus,
and lo, the Lord is with us, for we have perceived Him.

Yet all the time we live and move and have our being in a world of spiritual realities just as the blind man moves in a world of light ; it is spiritual senses that are lacking to us, not spiritual qualities to the universe.

It is because we persist in trying to use the faculties of the mind to perceive the things of the Spirit that we are turned empty away. We might as well try to listen to a picture or see a symphony. We are using the wrong sense-organs. They are not designed for the use to which we are trying to put them, hence our failure to see for ourselves what others tell us is there—we cannot find the bread of life for want of which our souls are starving because, metaphorically speaking, we listen for it instead of looking for it.

The mind is an organ of interpretation, not a sense-organ. It cannot directly apprehend the objective world, of whatever plane, and just as it must be served by sense-organs if it is to perceive the physical world, so it must be served by sense-organs if it is to perceive the spiritual world, and in this case its sense-organs are the spiritual emotions. What we *feel* concerning spiritual things the mind can interpret, but it cannot conceive what we have never felt.

But how are we to get our first glimpse of these transcendent spiritual realities for which we have no words and of which, having no concept, we cannot compare with things already known, and so arrive at some understanding of their nature ?

It was the work of Our Lord Jesus Christ to make the Kingdom of Heaven tangible to us so that there should be in human consciousness concepts of spiritual things, and He did it by translating spiritual ideas into physical actions.

He caused the sick to be healed, the hungry to be fed,

the sinful to be pardoned, the sorrowful to be comforted. These things are the fruits of the spirit, and the emotion we feel when we contemplate Our Lord's works is a spiritual emotion. Having felt it, we can begin to think about it, and when we think about it, we shall soon begin to arrive at some understanding of spiritual things.

THE THIRD SUNDAY IN ADVENT

" O Lord Jesus Christ, who at thy first coming didst send thy messenger to prepare thy way before thee ; grant that the ministers and stewards of thy mysteries may likewise so prepare and make ready thy way, by turning the hearts of the disobedient to the wisdom of the just, that at thy second coming to judge the world we may be found an acceptable people in thy sight, who livest and reignest with the Father and the Holy Spirit, ever one God, world without end. Amen."

KEYNOTE : SHOWING THE POWER OF GOD

Having ourselves learnt of the Master, how can we best bring others to meet Him ? We, who are working on the lines of mystical Christianity, have a more difficult problem to solve than those who have to give His message in its simpler forms. Mysticism will never appeal to the many. We must be careful not to force our views on souls who are not prepared for them by the wakening of the higher consciousness, and so disturb a simple faith that met their needs. Let us rather lead an inner life of living spiritual contacts, letting the light of those contacts shine through us. We do not sufficiently realise the power of the unspoken word. When we ourselves *feel* the power of the Master in our lives, we are transmitting that power, and others are very conscious of it.

Let our meditation this week be upon the power of the Christ-force to radiate out from us when we ourselves have contacted it, and let us strive to come into touch with the Master Jesus through prayer and aspiration, so that, having received power of Him, we can give to others. Unless we have so received, we have nothing to offer, for theology never comforted a heart in trouble.

THE FOURTH SUNDAY IN ADVENT

" O LORD, raise up (we pray thee) thy power, and come among us, and with great might succour us ; that whereas, through our sins and wickedness, we are sore let and hindered in running the race that is set before us, thy bountiful grace and mercy may speedily help and deliver us ; through the satisfaction of thy Son our Lord, to whom with thee and the Holy Ghost be honour and glory, world without end. Amen."

KEYNOTE : PURIFICATION

This collect starts with a tremendous invocation. How many are there who would dare to invoke the power of Christ to come among us if we realised what this invocation really meant ? Would we be willing for it to search our hearts and try us as gold is tried in the furnace ? Nevertheless, if we dare to so offer ourselves as channels for His power, and willingly undergo the purifying process that that power will exercise upon us at its first incoming ; parting readily with our dross, not seeking to justify ourselves, but rather to learn to see more clearly where our mistakes have been, then that power will most assuredly flow into us in response to the tremendous invocation of the fourth collect of Advent ; and from us, when the purificatory process has sufficiently opened the channel, it will flow on for the helping of the world.

24

Let us, therefore, in humility and self-sacrifice give ourselves as instruments for His work, and dare to offer the prayer, " O Lord, raise up Thy power and come among us."

CHRISTMAS DAY

" ALMIGHTY God, who hast given us thy only-begotten Son to take our nature upon him, and at this time to be born of a pure Virgin ; grant that we being regenerate, and made thy children by adoption and grace, may daily be renewed by thy Holy Spirit ; through the same our Lord Jesus Christ, who liveth and reigneth with thee and the same Spirit, ever one God, world without end. Amen."

KEYNOTE : BEGIN AT THE BEGINNING

The symbol of the Churches, teaching the multitude, is the Crucifix, the sacrificed Christ ; but the mystic knows the Risen Christ, ever-living, ever-working, His power flowing forth to all who invoke His Name. So also with the mystical interpretation of the Nativity ; the symbol of the Churches is the Christ-Child, laid in the manger, but the mystic knows the Christ-Idea, dimly realised in the newly awakened consciousness.

It is with the power of the Risen Christ that we work in mystical Christianity, and each one of us must awaken the Christ-power within ourselves by trying to live the Christ-life. It is the beauty of Christianity that although it can meet the loftiest intellectual needs, it is at the same time absolutely simple, because the Master, by living among us, showed us exactly what to do, for we have only to " live the life in order to know the doctrine."

As soon as ever we try to follow the example of the Master Jesus, we begin to understand Him.

Let us for our Christmas meditation take the thought of the little Christ-Child, not yet entered upon His mission as Messiah, not yet working with the power of the Holy Ghost, but who just lives in the home of His father, and simply loves and trusts.

We often fail to understand the Master through the living of the Christ-life because we forget that He began His earthly journey as a little child. We try and begin where He ended. If we were content to start by being little children in our relation to God, just living in the house of our Heavenly Father and loving and trusting, we could make a start in the great experience of spiritual realisation, and growth would soon follow.

SAINT STEPHEN'S DAY

" GRANT, O Lord, that, in all our sufferings here upon earth for the testimony of thy truth, we may steadfastly look up to heaven, and by faith behold the glory that shall be revealed ; and, being filled with the Holy Ghost, may learn to love and bless our persecutors by the example of thy first Martyr Saint Stephen, who prayed for his murderers to thee, O blessed Jesus, who standest at the right hand of God to succour all those that suffer for thee, our only Mediator and Advocate.   Amen."

KEYNOTE : FIDELITY TO OUR IDEALS

The first martyr in the Christian story is Saint Stephen, who was stoned to death because the ideal he upheld was felt as a rebuke by men who reckoned themselves righteous.

When we have to make the choice between spiritual principles and expediency, we must be prepared to make sacrifices. Men have always stoned those who have held up before their eyes a standard higher than they are prepared to accept. Adherence to spiritual principles is never going to give us the flesh-pots of Egypt. We must make up our minds to that before we set out on the journey to the Promised Land. If we are not prepared to live upon manna and depend upon the

Living Rock for water, we had better remain in bondage, for we shall die in the wilderness before the Promised Land is reached.

Like Saint Stephen, the first martyr, we must look steadfastly up into heaven if we are going to tread the Path, for it is there our treasure is. We must not expect to receive material rewards for spiritual work. When we love our enemies, we do not hope to win popularity thereby ; when we give all for Christ we do not expect to receive the best places in the synagogue. Our reward is to have been able, in some small measure, to lift the world's burden of sorrow and suffering inasmuch as we have transmuted hate into compassion and strife into gentleness.

When, with the stones falling all about us we hold steadfastly to the highest, then do we see the Heavens opened and the Son of Man standing on the right hand of God. Then there dawns upon us the power of mystical consciousness for which we toiled so long without visible result. Patiently, day by day, in prayer and service, we have sown the things of the spirit, and we have received the gifts of the spirit in joy, peace, and a sense of God's blessing. But the great experiences of the mystical life do not come until we have known crisis. The prayer for Divine Union is made in the shelter of the inner chamber behind the closed door, but it is answered when the winds of heaven blow in storm about the soul.

In that dark and stormy hour, let us try to rise into the higher consciousness ; serenely placing our life in God's hands ; compassionately and uncomplainingly meeting our adversaries ; with no feelings of bitterness towards those who have offered themselves as the channels of the suffering that falls to our portion. This indeed is the highest achievement of the Christian soul in its distress—that it does not pray to be saved, but asks that its persecutors may be pardoned and that it may draw nearer to the Master.

SAINT JOHN THE EVANGELIST'S DAY

" MERCIFUL Lord, we beseech thee to cast thy bright beams of light upon thy Church, that it being enlightened by the doctrine of thy blessed Apostle and Evangelist Saint John may so walk in the light of thy truth, that it may at length attain to the light of everlasting life ; through Jesus Christ our Lord. Amen."

KEYNOTE : DEEPER UNDERSTANDING

The simile of light, and all the words that derive therefrom, have ever been used when men seek to describe the change that takes place in human consciousness when spiritual forces begin to work upon it. The Mystic seeks Illumination, and his way is enlightened by the Inner Light.

There has always been this Inner Light for those who sought it—the understanding that transcends the intellect —the mode of mentation that transcends the reason. The fruits of this higher consciousness were gathered up into the Gnosis, and into the doctrine of the Illuminati— those intellectual mystics who have been most truly of the Company of Christ though seldom within the fold of the Church.

The writings attributed to Saint John bear the clear marks of a familiarity with the Greek Mystery schools and the mystical Qabbalism of Israel. The disciple whom Jesus loved was undoubtedly aware of the existence of a Secret Doctrine within the exoteric systems of the day.   It was concerning him that Our Lord said, while not denying that he should die even as other men, that nevertheless he should tarry till He came.   Saint John it is who has more to tell us concerning the Holy Ghost than any of the other Evangelists.

It is this Inner Light of mystical consciousness which must illumine the Church if it is to lead us from darkness to light, from death to life.   There is a deeper significance in Christianity than is contained in the rationalisations of theology or that realisation of spiritual truth which meets the needs of the wayfaring man.   Saint John, coming to Christianity from the illuminism of Greece and Israel, knew that there must always be a presentation of the teaching which should be available for simple souls, taught only by their hearts ; but there are abundant signs throughout the writings attributed to him which indicate his realisation of a potent spiritual power behind the simple revelation which was given to simple souls.

It is this deeper revelation which we need to-day if Christianity is to recover its lost influence over thinking men and women.   It is there, awaiting development. Christianity is very far from being a burnt-out cinder. Christianity must have a Gnosis as well as a creed. The mystic who rises into the higher consciousness on the wings of love alone has had much to give to the spiritual life of men, but we must also find a place for the mystic who rises to the higher consciousness on the wings of those rarer powers of the mind that have been known in the Mysteries from time immemorial.   We need our Christian Mysteries—the deeper teaching that cannot be given save after dedication and purification.

We need not only to know God as our Heavenly

Father but to understand Him as the creative Logos. Unless this aspect be rediscovered and reintroduced into Christianity, it will continue to be the faith of peasants and women, and the finest minds of our race will receive from it a stone when they ask for bread.

THE INNOCENTS' DAY

"O ALMIGHTY God, who out of the mouths of babes and sucklings hast ordained strength, and madest infants to glorify thee by their deaths; mortify and kill all vices in us, and so strengthen us by thy grace, that by the innocency of our lives, and constancy of our faith even unto death, we may glorify thy holy Name; through Jesus Christ our Lord. Amen."

KEYNOTE: "EXCEPT YE BECOME AS LITTLE CHILDREN——"

"God hath chosen the weak things of the world to confound the things that are mighty." It has never been those with the most powerful intellects who went furthest in the spiritual life, but those who had the clearest understanding of Our Lord's nature, who had the firmest grasp of spiritual principles, and who were prepared to act upon them at whatever cost. These have always been the "salt of the earth" even in the eyes of the worldly, and they have always been the ones whom time has justified.

A child, before its outlook becomes sophisticated, has a clear understanding of real values. In the character of a child of beautiful nature we see the nearest approximation to the Christian ideal. When we set out on the quest of spiritual reality we should bear this in mind, and remember that it is not with the powers of the mind that we shall perceive spiritual things, but rather with the powers of the heart.

We start our earthly journey as little children, and after passing by the flowery path of youth and the thorny path of maturity, we end it as little children. It is this child-spirit which catches glimpses of the Kingdom as we journey, and unless we can keep in our hearts the spirit of the child with which we set out, which came " trailing clouds of glory from heaven which is his home," we shall miss the biggest things in life, the profoundest truths of knowledge, the most beautiful things of art.

Let us strive to keep the spontaneity and simplicity of childhood throughout life's journey, for it is very near to the Kingdom. It is only the humble who can be helped. Those who are wise in their own conceit must go in their own strength.

THE SUNDAY AFTER CHRISTMAS DAY

" ALMIGHTY God, who hast given us thy only-begotten
Son to take our nature upon Him, and as at this time
to be born of a pure Virgin ; grant that we being regenerate, and made thy children by adoption and grace,
may daily be renewed by thy Holy Spirit ; through the
same our Lord Jesus Christ, who liveth and reigneth
with thee and the same Spirit, ever one God, world
without end.   Amen."

KEYNOTE : CHRIST THE REDEEMER

It is in his sense of an external reality expressed as
a Being that the Christian mystic differs from the
rationalist, however noble and idealistic his outlook.
The rationalist, holding just as lofty ideals as the
Christian, believes that no one and nothing can avail to
attain these ideals save his own unaided efforts, and that
the redemption of the world can only be achieved
through the united efforts of mankind.

The Christian says, The unaided efforts of mankind
would take too long to do the work of purifying and
perfecting the world.   Meanwhile, mankind, like a
creature that is penned but not tended, would die of its
own filth.   The cumulative effects of human error would

overcome the earth, even as in the old story of the sins of the sons of Adam.

We need help, and if we are wise, we will try not to go in our own strength but admit our need, and accept the help that is there, awaiting us. For God has not left us comfortless, but, knowing human frailty, has given us One who answers the call of the heart. When the cry for redemption goes forth into the deeps of the spirit, One comes in answer, One whom humanity can know and understand, for He was a man with men.

From Him we learn those qualities of the human character which enable the higher consciousness to dawn in the personality. Purified and exalted by experience of the Christ-force as transmitted by Our Lord, we can await in the upper chamber the coming of the Holy Ghost in tongues of living flame that shall illuminate the understanding.

Not until the gentle work of the Redeemer has been done in our hearts can we bear that fiery descent of mystical power that shall teach us all things.

THE CIRCUMCISION OF CHRIST

"ALMIGHTY God, who madest thy blessed Son to be circumcised, and obedient to the law for man ; grant us the true circumcision of the Spirit ; that our hearts and all our members, being mortified from all worldly and carnal lusts, we may in all things obey thy blessed will ; through the same thy Son Jesus Christ our Lord. Amen."

KEYNOTE : FULFILLING THE DUTIES OF LIFE

On the first day of the New Year the Church commemorates the Circumcision. This practice, so essential to the Jewish faith, was fulfilled by Our Lord, and yet Saint Paul says, " In Jesus Christ neither circumcision availeth anything, nor uncircumcision." Out of this seeming contradiction comes a very important practical lesson for us. The Master Jesus was not limited by any race prejudices, and yet He was always most careful to fulfil all the ritual requirements of the Jews and to " Render unto Cæsar the things that are Cæsar's." The Apostle Paul, on the other hand, " very Jew of very Jew," became the Apostle to the Gentiles and broke through the limitations of Jewish Orthodoxy.

If, however, we looked upon the Master as a reactionary and the Apostle as an anarchist, we should be far beside the mark, for each qualified his attitude. The

38

Master said, " The Sabbath was made for man, not man for the Sabbath ", and healed thereon in defiance of the prohibitions of the Law ; and Saint Paul, after the words we have quoted from Galatians v. 6, goes on to say that the thing which really avails is " faith which worketh by love."

Our Master taught His disciples that they had to be good Jews before they could be good Christians, and we have to be good men and women before we can hope to attain to a state of super-humanity.

Let us, therefore, take for our meditation this week The Fulfilling of the Duties of Daily Life. Just as the Church uses symbols to express spiritual things on the physical plane, so let us ever bear in mind that our earth-life is a symbol of the Spiritual Man, who is our real self. Every act we do in our daily routine can be sacramental for us if we make it so, and our daily toil become an exercise for the soul's growth. Let us, therefore, fulfil the Law in our homes, in our businesses, in our town, county and country. Let the mystic be a good citizen, and so follow the example of his Master, Who was a circumcised Jew before He was the Light of the World.

THE EPIPHANY

" O GOD, who by the leading of a star didst manifest thy only-begotten Son to the Gentiles ; mercifully grant, that we, which know thee now by faith, may after this life have the fruition of thy glorious Godhead ; through Jesus Christ our Lord. Amen."

KEYNOTE : SPIRITUAL DISCERNMENT

Like the Wise Men of the East who watched the stars, we are all looking for light from above to enlighten our darkness. By faith we believe in the evidence of things not seen, but can we grasp the substance of things hoped for ?

The Wise Men, led of the Star, came to the stable-cave near Bethlehem, and there they saw a child and its mother. To other eyes, that Child must have appeared as other new-born children. No one hastened to do It reverence, nor to comfort the Mother, lying amid the straw. But the Wise Men, taught of a deeper wisdom, saw otherwise as they knelt in that stable ; and such gifts as ambassadors bring to kings they offered to the Child lying in the hay, whom the other guests of the crowded inn passed by unnoticed.

Yet it was the same Child. The difference was in the observers. The Wise Men saw the Divinity hidden behind the veil of new-made flesh. Others saw nothing but the outer form.

So it is with the sacraments of the Church. Unless we have the seeing eye, taught of the higher illumination, we shall see no more than the hurrying servants saw as they passed through the stable at Bethlehem. We shall see nothing but empty forms in the traditional symbolic rituals of the Church. But if we can discern the things of the kingdom, we shall see that these forms, empty of intellectual or rational content though they be, are ensouled with the Christ-life.

It was to the great Being now incarnated that the Three Wise Men did reverence, not to the new-born Child the servants saw. So we, in the sacraments, should see the Christ incarnated in symbolism ; presented to our consciousness in a form which it can apprehend ; working by means of associated ideas to convey to our limited understanding a realisation of things which exceed its grasp.

The Epiphany means the viewing. Let us pray that we may come to the sacraments with the seeing eyes of the Wise Men, discerning the spirit that animates them ; and not, with the unheeding eyes of the hurrying servants, seeing nothing but the outer form.

THE FIRST SUNDAY AFTER EPIPHANY

" O LORD, we beseech thee mercifully to receive the prayers of thy people which call upon thee ; and grant that they may both perceive and know what things they ought to do, and also may have grace and power faithfully to fulfil the same ; through Jesus Christ our Lord. Amen."

KEYNOTE : COURAGE

In the wording of this collect we are given a valuable insight into the rationale of prayer. Most people, when they pray, ask God for the things they want ; they beg for their needs to be met ; for their burdens to be lifted from them and their way to be made straight before their feet by a divine intervention—an abrogation of the natural law of cause and effect—a miracle.

Not thus does the Church teach us to pray. " Grant that they may perceive and know what things they ought to do, and also may have grace and power faithfully to fulfil the same." Here is a noble prayer for wisdom and strength. We are not taught to ask that our burdens may be lifted, our problems solved, and our weakness and foolishness thereby condoned. We should ask for growth in understanding that we may discern clearly and judge wisely ; we should ask for strength that shall enable us to go through our difficulties and master them once and for all, coming out of the ordeal with ennobled characters ; we should not ask for mercy that shall enable us to evade them, passing on with the lesson they could teach omitted from our experience. This courageous and beautiful prayer should be the daily and hourly prayer of all who are in trouble, asking, like the old saint, not " for tasks according to our strength, but for strength according to our tasks."

God does not lead us unto the wilderness to perish. There is grace through Our Lord Jesus Christ for the solution of every problem God sets us. Does a teacher set a child a problem in geometry and then leave him to his own devices ? No. He says, " If you cannot understand this, come and ask me," and he will patiently explain until the child understands. What would his attitude be towards the child who begged him of his mercy to spare him this problem ? Would he not say, " You must understand the principles involved before you can do any more work in geometry. It would be no kindness to you if I allowed you to pass it by uncompleted, for at every turn you would find yourself meeting the same problem in other forms, and you would still be baffled. Come now, let us see whether, with my help, you cannot solve it. I am well aware that it appears insoluble to you at present, but see, I will explain it to you."

Thus says Our Lord to us when we are in trouble, " See, I will explain it to you—Now go and work it out." In the light of the spirit that was in Christ Jesus, every problem that God sets us can be solved.

THE SECOND SUNDAY AFTER EPIPHANY

" ALMIGHTY and everlasting God, who dost govern all things in heaven and earth ; mercifully hear the supplications of thy people, and grant us thy peace all the days of our life ; through Jesus Christ our Lord. Amen."

KEYNOTE : " GRANT US THY PEACE "

" Grant us thy peace all the days of our life," say the beautiful words of the collect. To whom is this prayer directed ? Under what aspect does it invoke the Deity ? It is addressed to the " Almighty and everlasting God, who dost govern all things in heaven and earth." It invokes God as natural law.

God and natural law are one and the same. For what is natural law save the observed sequence of events ? And upon what does the sequence of events depend save the innate nature of things ? And what is the innate nature of things save God's nature manifesting itself in His creation ?

But natural law does very much more than " bring forth Mazzaroth in his season and guide Arcturus with his sons." It rules the realms of mind and mental power—of thought as causation and of emotion and instinct as vital factors in the affairs of men and nations. All these things, subtle but potent, are ruled by law ;

44

they are part of the creation of God who is Spirit. The significance of this fact is recognised by those who study the power of the mind to heal human ills and solve human troubles.

The words of the collect indicate clearly the way we should go if we desire peace all the days of our life—we should seek to understand and observe the laws of God which govern the universe on all its planes, on the hidden mind-side of things as well as their external matter-aspect. We shall find the necessary guidance in the pages of Scripture. Our Bible is the Book of the Laws of the Unseen Forces. If we study its pages we shall learn all we need to know concerning the way in which the mind acts as intermediary between spirit and matter.

If we want to have health all the days of our life we observe the rules of physical hygiene. If we want to have peace all the days of our life we must observe the rules of spiritual hygiene. We must refrain from breaking the spiritual laws of the mind, and bring every thought into captivity to Christ Jesus. Otherwise, if we indulge in lawless thinking, we shall be setting causes in motion which will bring us discord instead of peace.

God's law prevails upon every plane of existence and must be kept, otherwise there befalls us the consequences of the breaking of a natural law—disharmony and disruption. We cry that God has afflicted us and pray for mercy ; or that the devil is tormenting us, and pray for protection ; whereas we ourselves, by our own wrong thinking and feeling, are breaking the natural laws of the spiritual realm.

THE THIRD SUNDAY AFTER EPIPHANY

" ALMIGHTY and everlasting God, mercifully look upon our infirmities, and in all our dangers and necessities stretch forth thy right hand to help and defend us ; through Jesus Christ our Lord. Amen."

KEYNOTE : LOOK WITHIN

This prayer for help in need and protection in danger has for its opening words an appeal for mercy towards our own shortcoming. In all difficulties we should always look first into our own hearts. It does not matter how wrongly other people may be acting, let us put all they have done out of our minds, for it will only obscure the issue, and ask ourselves first and foremost, are we, in the light of our own knowledge of the power of the mind and the spiritual laws that govern it, handling rightly our own reactions ? Are we controlling our feelings so that we maintain our courage and compassion undisturbed whatever may be happening in the outer world ? Is the peace of God indeed abiding in our hearts and minds ? It is for us to seek that peace and ensue it by maintaining in ourselves the mind that was also in Christ Jesus.

It is our own infirmities alone that expose us to spiritual danger. Our Heavenly Father is not an " Agent

46

provocateur." He does not deliberately lead us into temptation. When we send out our thoughts in aspiration and invocation towards Him, spiritual force pours down upon us, and the effect of that force is to stimulate into reaction everything in our nature that is incompatible with Its purity and goodness. It is this reaction which is the Temptation that follows the Baptism.

If our own infirmities receive mercy, we have little need to trouble about the spiritual dangers that assail us from without. Nothing can harm us except our own reactions. "Fear not them which kill the body but are not able to kill the soul; but fear rather him that is able to destroy both body and soul in hell." Who is this evil genius? Nothing and no one but our own lower self.

THE FOURTH SUNDAY AFTER EPIPHANY

" O God, who knowest us to be set in the midst of so many and great dangers, that by reason of the frailty of our nature we cannot always stand upright ; grant to us such strength and protection, as may support us in all dangers, and carry us through all temptations ; through Jesus Christ our Lord. Amen."

KEYNOTE : PROTECTION FROM EVIL

Although we may recognise the need for precaution in times of danger, let us never forget that our strongest weapon is courage. No influence or attack, however strong, can ever injure the soul unless we allow ourselves to vibrate in response to its note. The best method of defence is to hold consciousness steady by tuning it to a definite keynote and keeping it vibrating at that pitch all the time by constant meditation. Once again the collect gives us the keynote in teaching us to pray for the help we need to be sent us " through Jesus Christ our Lord."

" By reason of the frailty of our nature we cannot always stand upright," says the old prayer, and who does not know its truth ? When spiritual evil threatens, we have nothing to fear except ourselves. As long as we can keep our hearts and minds fixed steadily on Christ

48

Jesus, so that His influence permeates our whole being, we shall not react to the forces of evil, and evil will be powerless to harm us.

It is not the evil which assails the soul that injures us, but the evil that finds entrance into the soul.

We may wonder why it is that when we are sincerely striving after spiritual things the fiercest assaults of evil should fall upon us. There is always a backwash with every tide. The flowing tide of spiritual force stirs up the powers of evil ; we must be prepared for this when we enter upon the spiritual life ; it is no strange thing which befalls us ; all the servants of God have known it.

There are forces in the Unseen which are but little understood ; the sheep of Christ's flock, the souls who look to Him as Shepherd, not as Master, are protected from these forces ; they are not called upon to encounter them. But we, if we elect to follow the straight way to the heights, if we would aspire to work with Our Master in His tasks and not merely to be carried in His bosom, must be prepared to encounter those forces and conditions which Saint Paul referred to as " Spiritual wickedness in high places."

Let us never forget that it is " by reason of the frailty of our nature that we cannot always stand upright." Let us watch our own thoughts closely when we are encountering the dark storms of the spiritual world, for it is here that the first danger shows itself. And let our thoughts be so centred about Our Lord, so filled and imbued with love and faith, that evil, and the fear that opens the door to evil, can find no cranny for a lodging-place.

THE FIFTH SUNDAY AFTER EPIPHANY

" O LORD, we beseech thee to keep thy Church and household continually in thy true religion ; that they who do lean only upon the hope of thy heavenly grace may evermore be defended by thy mighty power ; through Jesus Christ our Lord. Amen."

KEYNOTE: FIDELITY TO CHRIST'S STANDARD

The collect for this Sunday teaches us to pray for guidance in our perception of spiritual truth ; it is not enough that there should be an original mandate, inspiration, or source of teaching, we must be kept " continually " in the way of truth if we are to arrive safely at the goal of Divine Union without wandering by the way.

We do not realise sufficiently the need for " continual " revision of our standpoint ; we do not realise how liable we are to err without knowing it. It is a fact well known to those who train the blind in handicrafts that no blind worker, however skilled, can work long without supervision ; his workmanship unconsciously deteriorates because he has no means of judging that which he has done ; so it is with us who, still hooded by brain-consciousness, try to work on the higher planes ; unless we have help from the Master, our work tends to deteriorate. This is a phenomenon well known to all followers of the Mystic Way.

Let us, therefore, set this week aside to ask for help from the Master in revising our standard of work lest it fall from its high ideal and we become limited, prejudiced or stereotyped in our outlook. Let us constantly meditate on the Beatitudes so that we may not depart from the " pattern shown us in the Mount "—so that we may not drop down from the exalted consciousness which enabled us to glimpse the spiritual ideal that started us off on our quest.

In the Epistle for this day, Saint Paul counsels us to " humbleness of mind " : without this quality there can be no perception of new truths nor revision of old ones ; it is essential to spiritual advancement. Let us be continually measuring our own achievements and under-standing against those of the great Masters of the Inner Life, the saints and seers. By so doing we shall obtain a sense of perspective and proportion. If we constantly associate in our reading with those who have achieved, not being content with any rendering of their teaching or attempted simplification of their message, but going direct to their own words for our guidance and inspira-tion, we shall find that we are insensibly moulded to their viewpoint, and thereby our feet are set on the right path.

From their self-doubting, which crops up continually, we shall learn the need of the " humbleness of mind " which Saint Paul, one of the very greatest of the Masters of the Inner Life, is forever emphasising. The greater the inrush of the spirit into the soul, the more does it realise the limitations of the mind ; the greater the realisation of the grandeur of the world of the spirit, the more does it distrust its own power to apprehend it ;

but out of this distrust comes, not paralysis, but perception ; for the soul, reaching its limit, becomes still and awaits the Master, and in that stillness does He come.

Let our keynote for the week's meditation be : Master, keep me *continually* in Thy true religion.

THE SIXTH SUNDAY AFTER EPIPHANY

" O GOD, whose blessed Son was manifested that he might destroy the works of the devil, and make us the sons of God, and heirs of eternal life ; grant us, we beseech thee, that, having this hope, we may purify ourselves, even as he is pure ; that, when he shall appear again with power and great glory, we may be made like unto him in his eternal and glorious kingdom ; where with thee, O Father, and thee, O Holy Ghost, he liveth and reigneth, ever one God, world without end. Amen."

KEYNOTE : PURIFICATION

Saint Paul counsels us " to bring every thought into captivity to Christ Jesus." This means that not only must the thoughts we deliberately formulate be Christ-like, but even the imaginations which rise from the depths of our hearts. How is this to be achieved ? Constant vigilance alone will not suffice.

If a sculptor be carving a statue, he constantly looks up from his work to the model he is trying to represent. All artists recognise that it is essential that they should work from the living model, otherwise they tend to reproduce what they imagine they have seen, not what is actually there.

So it is with us when we strive after spiritual

perfection. A living model is essential to us, otherwise we shall fall into error unknowingly. This model we have in Him who has been so truly called our Great Exemplar. To the contemplation of character as shown forth in His Life we must continually return ; otherwise we shall surely lose sight of our ideal.

Unless we continually raise consciousness to spiritual things, we tend to lose touch with them. The thousand calls of the world, coming to us through the gates of the senses, cause us to focus our attention upon mundane things. The still, small voice of the Spirit is not heard amid the distractions of daily life unless we deliberately set aside a period in which we shall enter into the Silence and listen to it.

The more we have to do, the more the pressure of the world closes in upon us, the more do we need to be resolute in reserving a period of each day for communion with God. Whatever else has to be crowded out, let us cling to those few minutes apart in the Silence ; it is hard to conceive any circumstances in which they cannot be obtained if resolutely sought.

SEPTUAGESIMA SUNDAY

" O LORD, we beseech thee favourably to hear the
prayers of thy people ; that we, who are justly punished
for our offences, may be mercifully delivered by thy
goodness, for the glory of thy Name ; through Jesus
Christ our Saviour, who liveth and reigneth with thee
and the Holy Ghost, ever one God, world without end.
Amen."

KEYNOTE : FORGIVENESS OF SINS

It is easier to conceive that our Heavenly Father will
help us out of our troubles than that we are justly
punished for our offences and have to look to ourselves
for help—have to change our ways of thinking before
conditions can change for us. If we realised the enormous
power of thought, we should see that the imaginings of
our hearts, when every thought has not been brought
into captivity to Christ Jesus, are the true fountain-head
of our sorrows.

We must not be content with making clean the outside
of the golden bowl, leaving all uncleanness within.
Repressed desires that have been prevented by circumstances from achieving their ends, though impotent on
the physical plane, are nevertheless potent on the spiritual
plane. If these be unregenerate, they will assuredly bring
forth the fruits of sin, which is death. If we applied to
our spiritual life some of the knowledge which a deeper

understanding of the human mind is bringing to light, we might get an insight into the nature of much suffering which we fondly believed to be vicarious.

It is true that no man can see into his own sub-conscious mind, but we may rest assured that the Old Adam dwells there in ourselves as in others unless we have wrought ourselves into the likeness of the New Adam, which is Christ Jesus. Racial habits will hold unless the regenerated consciousness has changed them.

The Sacrifice of the Cross was made by the Christ for the human race, and we share in it as we share in the evolving life of our species ; but the Master Jesus can only become our personal Saviour, can only regenerate our personalities, in proportion as He is our Exemplar. " Can you drink the Cup that I drink of, and be baptised with the baptism that I am baptised with ? " said the Master to those who asked if they might sit at His side in glory. The Way-shower can only save us if we tread the Way He shows.

SEXAGESIMA SUNDAY

" O LORD God, who seest that we put not our trust in any thing that we do ; mercifully grant that by thy power we may be defended against all adversity ; through Jesus Christ our Lord. Amen."

KEYNOTE : " BE STILL AND KNOW THAT I AM GOD "

People sometimes take exception to the prayers of the Church because they feel them to be servile in tone and derogatory to the dignity of human free-will. If, with the old anthropomorphic concept we look upon God as a magnified despotic king, this would undoubtedly be the case ; but when we realise that what we uncomprehendingly call God is the Logoidal Consciousness which has projected this universe as a thought-form, we understand the significance these prayers have for souls with spiritual insight.

All mystics know that they can only go a certain distance upon the Path, and then they have to be still and listen for the coming of a Presence which is not of this plane of existence. The candidate has to await the Great Initiator. This experience is more than a subjective realisation ; something from without acts upon us, and if it acts not, then nothing happens. It is this meeting with the Beloved which the mystic seeks as he raises consciousness to the higher planes. He finds his Master through love, and his initiation is an experience of union through love with his beloved Master. The mystics of every path, Catholic, Quaker, Sufi, Buddhist, Hindu, Taoist have all borne witness to this, and in the testimony of many witnesses there is truth.

Let us for our work in meditation this week try to be still and feel God all about us ; let us realise that our individual lives are part of the great One Life which brought us into being and forever sustains and holds us in Its love. Let us remember that we live in this One Life and not in any separate struggling existence of our own ; it is only a delusion of the senses to think that we have to maintain our separate existences, we simply have to " Be still, and know that I am God."

QUINQUAGESIMA SUNDAY

" O LORD, who hast taught us that all our doings without charity are nothing worth ; send thy Holy Ghost, and pour into our hearts that most excellent gift of charity, the very bond of peace and of all virtues, without which whosoever liveth is counted dead before thee ; grant this for thine only Son Jesus Christ's sake. Amen."

KEYNOTE : COMPASSION

The word which the Authorised Version of the Scriptures translates as charity is rendered in the Revised Version as Love. If this word be substituted, we shall realise the full beauty of this collect and the Epistle which follows it.

" Love never faileth," says Saint Paul. " Whether there be prophecies, they shall fail ; whether there be tongues, they shall cease ; whether there be knowledge, it shall vanish away." Paul, the learned doctor of Israel, enumerates the powers of the intellect and declares that they are as nothing beside the great gift of love.

Souls in the Outer Court are under the discipline of loving service, but the soul that penetrates to the Inner Court of mystic consciousness knows that there is another kind of love which is as much higher than the love of service as that love is higher than the personal love of the passions ; there is the Task of Mary as well as the Task of Martha, and in the Inner Court of uplifted consciousness, we sit at the Feet of the Master and are still in silent love ; it is this stillness of love which brings the realisation of His Nature, not the bustling of Martha in the kitchen. Although the task of service is a necessary stage upon the Path, it is not the highest stage, but one we leave behind when we have served our time therein. Too much *doing* and not enough *being* are a mistake upon the Path. It is the stillness of adoration that brings illumination. It is not enough that we should love the Master and that our enthusiasm should go out to Him and we should long to work for Him and learn from Him ; before we win to illumination we must have reached the stage when our realisation of the Master's nature and task shall have so overwhelmed us that we are unable to stir, even for service, but sit dumb and overcome at His Feet, made negative by His tremendous force, with His emanations suffusing us. Some mystics are afraid of becoming negative in their meditations, but it is only when we become receptive to the inflowing force of the Master that He can illuminate us. Those who kneel before God can stand before kings. The intellectualist too often forgets to worship. We must needs bow before the Highest when it touches our souls.

Love is the link between Master and disciple ; without it, whosoever liveth is counted as dead before Him. This love must be twofold : with one hand the seeker must reach up towards the Master, and with the other he must reach out towards his fellow-creatures, for the loving Master can only come unto us in proportion as we are loving. It is impossible to fill a vessel already full ; only as we pour out our love to others can God's love flow into our hearts ; if we live to ourselves, our life stagnates.

The beauty and profundity of this great lesson of love heralds the beginning of Lent, the season set aside by the Church for heart-searching. If our heart-searching reveals to us depths from which we feel we could never rise, let us turn back to this collect and the Epistle that follows it and remember that " much was forgiven to her because she had loved much," for " Love covereth a multitude of sins."   When the wise Rabbi was given the privilege of choosing what the Recording Angel should enter in the Book of Judgment against his name, he said, " Write me as one who loved his fellow-men."

For our meditation this week let us ask God for the gift of compassion and understanding, even if we can only win to understanding by ourselves knowing the need for compassion.

ASH WEDNESDAY

' ALMIGHTY and everlasting God, who hatest nothing that thou hast made, and dost forgive the sins of all them that are penitent ; create and make in us new and contrite hearts, that we worthily lamenting our sins, and acknowledging our wretchedness, may obtain of thee, the God of all mercy, perfect remission and forgiveness ; through Jesus Christ our Lord. Amen."

KEYNOTE : SELF-EXAMINATION

With this day we enter upon the most important season of the Church's year, the long purification which prepares for the down-pouring of power at Easter. Our task during Lent is to face ourselves, bring our natures under discipline, and make ready for the illumination that comes with the Easter power-tides.

People are sometimes estranged from the Church by what they feel to be the abject tone of some of her prayers, by their insistence upon the sinfulness and help-lessness of man, and his powerlessness without Divine aid. Let us try and realise that these prayers are written in an older form of English than that which is in use among us at the present day, and try to understand their spirit rather than resent their wording. If we read other books written at the same time as the Prayer Book, we should find ourselves in a similar difficulty.

The collect for Ash Wednesday presents two ideas for our meditation, firstly, the concept expressed in the beautiful phrase, " Almighty and everlasting God, who hatest nothing that thou hast made, and dost forgive the sins of all them that are penitent." Here we get a realisation of the distinction that is drawn between the sin and the sinner. It is the sin, the error, with which the spiritual forces deal as they maintain the cosmic balance, and the one who errs, if he persists in his error, may become involved in that adjustment and be ground exceeding fine in the mills of God ; but *all* who are penitent, all who turn again, are forgiven, that is to say, are harmonised with God. It is the sin which is destroyed, not the sinner.

Again, we get a clear realisation in this collect that we have no right to hate any soul, whatever may be its condition. We may not condone evil, we must stand up fearlessly for principles, but we must not hate. We must never uncover evil unless we have the means of healing it ; to hold a soul up to scorn serves no useful purpose.

The second idea presented to us by this collect emphasises the need for recognising our own short-comings. We must be our own judges, and the sentence that we pronounce on ourselves when we commence our Lenten meditation we must carry out during the forty days in the wilderness upon which we are now entering.

If we observe our lives, we shall find that a period of self-condemnation and abasement almost invariably precedes a period of flowing spiritual power. This self-disgust must be carefully distinguished from discontent with our circumstances or mere depression. We realise in this spiritual assessment that the problem lies within, and that no change of circumstances could amend it ; secondly, far from being weakened by our feelings, we are roused to activity, being thoroughly angry with ourselves, and this anger and self-disgust begets a determination not to fall again, and so earn our own self-contempt. There is nothing abject about true repentance, it is an energetic rising up of the nature to do better.

A recognition of sin is not a falling down flat of the soul in a grovelling attitude ; it is the soul that is sinning that is grovelling. Recognition is the exact opposite of this supine condition, for it is an uprising of the soul. I always think of the repentant sinner as standing bolt upright, shoulders squared, feet firmly planted, looking the Master straight in the eyes and admitting his error like a man. To admit the wrong, shoulder the conse- quences, and resolutely set out at all costs to return to the Path gives us the right to hold up our heads and claim the respect of our fellow-men, from whatever pit of abasement we may have to climb, and the Father, Who sees us afar off, always comes to meet us.

THE FIRST SUNDAY IN LENT

" O LORD, who for our sake didst fast forty days and forty nights ; give us grace to use such abstinence, that, our flesh being subdued to the Spirit, we may ever obey thy godly motions in righteousness and true holiness, to thy honour and glory, who livest and reignest with the Father and the Holy Ghost, one God, world without end. Amen."

KEYNOTE : SELF-DISCIPLINE

The keynote of this meditation is self-discipline, the body being brought into subjection in order that the higher self may come into full and free manifestation on the physical plane.

" The good I would, I do not ; and the evil that I would not, that I do," is a condition which must be overcome upon the probationary Path, there must be no involuntary movements when we are climbing the path " narrow as the edge of a razor." Therefore it is that all the saints and mystics of all traditions, without exception, have practised ascetic discipline in some degree.

Those voluntary exercises of the will are devised for the twofold purpose of strengthening the will itself and training the bodily appetites to take denial without undue protest. Self-inflicted suffering can never be pleasing to God as such, and if it is undertaken for that end it defeats itself, weakening the body and unbalancing the mind ; it is not the blood of rams, still less the suffering of His children that is an acceptable sacrifice to the God Who is Love, but rather the dedicated will ; but the will cannot be dedicated unless it is disciplined.

The small self-denials which are customary among practising Christians during Lent, Ember Days and Fridays throughout the year are the gymnastics of the soul, and keep it strong and supple to meet the sudden crises that test its stamina.

This week, then, let us make up our minds to dedicate to God the body and its needs, the instincts and their desires, and all that comprises the lower nature ; let us "Marry effort to desire," and make a start upon the training of the will that shall enable us to realise our ideals in our lives.

THE SECOND SUNDAY IN LENT

" ALMIGHTY God, who seest that we have no power of
ourselves to help ourselves ; keep us both outwardly in
our bodies, and inwardly in our souls ; that we may be
defended from all adversities which may happen to the
body, and from all evil thoughts which may assault and
hurt the soul ; through Jesus Christ our Lord. Amen."

KEYNOTE : WE SHINE WITH REFLECTED
LIGHT

The realisation that " we have no power of ourselves "
is the beginning of omnipotence.

Many people will no doubt take exception to the
statement in this collect that " we have no power of
ourselves to help ourselves," but it has a profound
significance, and the consequences of a failure to realise
this fundamental truth are all about us in the many
organisations that seek to give new forms to old
truths.

" Unless the Lord keep the house the watchman
waketh in vain." We do not live with our own life, but
because there is at the heart of each one of us a Divine
Spark from the Central Fire which is God.

It is by this one Divine Spark that we live ; through it,
we are part of the God-life ; it is indestructible in its

existence and unlimited in the spiritual power that can be drawn through it. Did we but realise its significance we should be as gods in the true sense, for the God-life would be awake within us.

Those prayers of the Church which stress the helplessness and hopelessness of man in a way derogatory to the pride of human nature are really indicating the path to the innermost shrine of the Temple, and it is not until we have an actual realisation of all the practical implications of the statement, " Your life is hid with Christ in God," and " He who will lose his life for My sake shall find it," that we shall be able to tread that Path.

In such a realisation we do not throw ourselves passively on the hands of a beneficent Providence, but invoke Omnipotence to flow through our consciousness where hitherto self-will and desire have had their channels. In order to achieve this, the lower self, which draws its strength from the instincts, must stand absolutely aside in order that the flow of the current of life may be reversed, for the Divine Life, instead of coming to us by what are popularly called natural means, is to come to us direct.

Let it not be thought that this is an unnatural process ; it is no more unnatural than an eclipse ; but it is rare, and but few can achieve it, and even they can only maintain it as long as the higher consciousness is functioning. That is why the saints of the mystic tradition record great tides of power and light and corresponding periods of darkness and aridity, for they, denying themselves the consolations of human life, are left desolate when the channel of the Divine flow is closed by the weaknesses that are ever with us until the final goal be reached.

It is here that training in the technique of the mystical life is of such value, for it enables us to maintain a balance that shall preserve us from the extremes of aridity and ecstasy ; teaching us to contact indirectly when we cannot contact directly.

THE THIRD SUNDAY IN LENT

" WE beseech thee, Almighty God, look upon the hearty desires of thy humble servants, and stretch forth the right hand of thy Majesty to be our defence against all our enemies ; through Jesus Christ our Lord. Amen."

KEYNOTE : " CAST OUT THE BEAM THAT IS IN THINE OWN EYE "

Here we have, though expressed in metaphor drawn from a primitive phase of the tradition of Israel, an invocation of the power of God.

" Be still and know that I am God," represents the height of moral power, and only the strong can rise to it, for that " stilling " of desire, anger, and fear is a supreme achievement of the disciplined soul. In this prayer the soul does not attempt the high places of spiritual attainment, but rather invokes the power of God to work upon the problems of daily life. It necessarily follows upon this that the law of God must also work upon these problems, and when we invoke God's power upon our " hearty desires " and the issue between ourselves and those we feel to be our enemies, we are going to the very roots of the matter, and " He will turn and overturn till he whose right it is shall reign," and we must be prepared to find that it may not be our right to reign and that we must sacrifice our " hearty desires " and make restitution to our enemies.

How many of us, when we pray to God for protection, ask also to be cleansed of our own errors ? We think in our blindness that if the attack from without could be stopped, there would be peace in the city. Does experience show this to be the case ? Alas, no.

The City of Mansoul, putting her trust in God, has impregnable fortifications ; it is treachery alone that opens the gate. Could malice harm us if we did not resent it ? Slander can do little to harm a pure, upright and gentle nature. Its inherent integrity is its defence ; mankind is not so blind that it cannot discern character. Our weakness in the face of an unwarranted attack lies in descending to the level of the attackers. If we remain steadfastly within our fortress of uplifted spiritual consciousness and refuse to be tempted forth to give battle on the plains, no one can penetrate into our city.

If, on the other hand, being attacked with malice, we respond with malice, we have opened the gates to our enemies, and fighting is taking place in the streets of our city. Whoever wins in the long run, we suffer damage.

Therefore let us pray to be cleansed from inner weaknesses as well as defended from external attack ; without this cleansing, no effectual defence is possible, for by our weaknesses we open ourselves to the attacks we dread. " In quietness and in confidence shall be your strength " when " the blast of the terrible ones is as the storm against the wall."

For this week, then, let those who are prepared to abide the issue and follow the right, whatever it may turn out to be, invoke the power of God upon their " hearty desires " and their enemies equally ; they may see unexpected changes ; they may find there is a price to pay ; but they will come out into green pastures and in the end will be at peace.

THE FOURTH SUNDAY IN LENT

" GRANT, we beseech thee, Almighty God, that we, who
for our evil deeds do worthily deserve to be punished,
by the comfort of thy grace may mercifully be relieved ;
through our Lord and Saviour Jesus Christ.   Amen."

KEYNOTE : EXPIATION BY REALISATION

In this collect we meet with a very profound aspect
of the Law of Redemption, wherein are utilised the
workings of Divine Grace for the ab-reaction of evil.
We are very apt to feel that the consequence of wrong is
a thing that has to be endured to the bitter end and
cannot be influenced or eased ; whereas, every time a
true spiritual healing is accomplished, the burden of sin
is lifted.

This is brought about in two ways : firstly, by the
soul's realisation of its problems and its needs, and
secondly by the force referred to in the collect as the
Grace of God.

To explain anything of the nature and workings of
this force would require very much more space than can
be assigned to a meditation ; indeed, it is doubtful
whether any explanation could be adequate, for like
electricity, we know this force rather for what it does
than for what it is.   It must suffice to say that a prayer
for God's grace brings a very powerful response.   A

force works upon the soul, uplifting it into a sense of power and freedom. That which was obscure becomes clear to consciousness ; that which was entangled becomes straight. The experiment has only to be made with the powerful invocation of faith in the Name of Our Lord Jesus Christ for it to be found that a force has been set in action.

In our struggles with the burden of our errors and the weakness of our characters, let us invoke the help of God's grace instead of trying to go in our own strength.

For this week, then, let us meditate upon the power of God working on our souls ; strengthening our weaknesses, cleansing our impurities, enlightening our understanding, and vivifying our love. This power we invoke is not any power of our own nature, not any power of created existence, but an emanation of the Divine Mind " in Whom we live and move and have our being."

When we realise that we do not live by any separate existence of our own, but as part of the One Life which is God ; when we realise that an intensification of this ever-inflowing Life can be produced by dwelling upon It in thought and calling upon It with the invocatory power of the knowledge of Its reality and potency, we shall find that a great load is lifted from our shoulders ; life will be eased of its strain, for we shall learn that our own character and its reactions are the only problems we have to contend with ; all else is ruled by the Divine Law, which ordereth all things harmoniously. If we bring our thoughts, feelings, and the reactions that spring from them into obedience to the Divine Law, we too shall, by Its omnipotent power, be tuned into harmony in mind, body and estate.

THE FIFTH SUNDAY IN LENT

" WE beseech thee, Almighty God, mercifully to look upon thy people ; that by thy great goodness they may be governed and preserved evermore, both in body and soul ; through Jesus Christ our Lord. Amen."

KEYNOTE : GOD OUR FATHER

The roots of our being must be in God. " In Him we live and move and have our being." God is the beginning and end of our existence, and His Nature is our law. Always must we come back to the One Existence. Always must we seek to align ourselves with the cosmic law that " guideth Arcturus with his sons." Not otherwise can we find harmony. If we understand prayer aright we shall know that God does not give us peace in answer to our prayer, but that by our prayer we bring ourselves into harmony with God and then the " peace of God which passeth all understanding " fills our hearts.

When God governs and preserves us we are at peace. Why then is it that we are ever disturbed, for we can never escape from His governance, and His preservation is our very existence ? We can never pass beyond the reign of His law ; all the time are we governed and preserved. The inharmony exists only in our lack of realisation and our fear.

Our prayer to God to govern and preserve us is

really a reminder to ourselves that we should wake
up from our dream of distress and realise that " under-
neath are the everlasting arms," and that " neither
height nor depth nor any other creature can separate us
from the love of God."

THE SUNDAY NEXT BEFORE EASTER

" ALMIGHTY and everlasting God, who, of thy tender love towards mankind, hast sent thy Son, our Saviour Jesus Christ, to take upon him our flesh, and to suffer death upon the Cross, that all mankind should follow the example of his great humility ; mercifully grant, that we may both follow the example of his patience, and also be made partakers of his resurrection ; through the same Jesus Christ our Lord. Amen."

KEYNOTE : "TAKE UP THY CROSS AND FOLLOW ME"

This collect teaches us to follow the example of the Master in order that we may be partakers of His resurrection. The soul goes through its crucifixion in order that it may preach to the spirits in prison.

With this collect we pray that we may drink of His Cup. It is not a prayer to be lightly used. But few souls can go by the Way of the Cross in its mystical sense, but all can use their experience of life as a means of helping others. Let our own sufferings teach us sympathy. Let our own limitations teach us mercy. Let our own impurities, as we hope for forgiveness ourselves, teach us to call nothing unclean beyond redemption.

We may not be able to " give our bodies to be burned,"

but we can have the charity which " suffereth long and is kind."

We may not be able to feed the five thousand, but we can give a cup of cold water where it is needed. Let us take for our meditation this week the task of being Christ-like in little things, for this is the beauty of holiness.

GOOD FRIDAY. I

" ALMIGHTY God, we beseech thee graciously to behold this thy family, for which our Lord Jesus Christ was contented to be betrayed, and given up into the hands of wicked men, and to suffer death upon the Cross, who now liveth and reigneth with thee and the Holy Ghost, ever one God, world without end. Amen."

KEYNOTE: THE LOVE OF BRETHREN

The collect of the most tragic commemoration of the Christian year contains no note of grief, but speaks of us as God's " family," for whose sake Our Lord suffered and triumphed. We ask the Heavenly Father " graciously to behold this thy family." It is a beautiful concept and links us closely to our Elder Brother, " the first-born of many brethren," Who has " gone before us into Galilee."

If we really felt that all God's children were one big family how differently we should act. If we felt towards the stranger that is within our gate and the brother at the ends of the earth whom we have never seen as if they were our loved ones, would it not bring the Kingdom of Heaven on earth ? Let us take for our meditation on this day, which commemorates the great sacrifice of Our Lord, the words, " Little children, I would that you should love one another." If we can only achieve that,

78

His sacrifice will not have been in vain. "God so loved the world that He gave His only-begotten Son that we should not perish, but have everlasting life." Is it too much to ask that we should love one another even as little children of the same family ?

GOOD FRIDAY. II

" ALMIGHTY and everlasting God, by whose Spirit the whole body of the Church is governed and sanctified ; receive our supplications and prayers, which we offer before thee for all estates of men in thy holy Church, that every member of the same, in his vocation and ministry, may truly and godly serve thee ; through our Lord and Saviour Jesus Christ. Amen."

KEYNOTE : THE WORK OF THE LAITY

The priests of the Roman Church have behind them the unceasing prayers of the encloistered Orders. The convents and monasteries of Contemplatives who undertake no active work for God in the world are by no means abodes of idleness and inaction, but rather power-houses of spiritual energy.

Why should not our own clergy have in the prayers of the faithful a similar source of support ? The power of organised prayer is very great. And not only is there the moral support of the knowledge that they are being " backed up " in their work, but certain little-known laws of the spiritual life come into operation, with very tangible results. A " circuit " is formed, and power flows therein.

The priest, if he be true priest and not a parson (from the Latin, *persona*, a mask), will be much in prayer over

his work ; but the effect of regular, organised prayer on
the part of his flock, not a perfunctory repetition of set
forms, but an earnest outpouring of spiritual energy, will
prove in the highest degree inspiring and sustaining.

Priest and people, acting and reacting on each other,
can lift each other to great heights. For although God's
grace is the source of all spiritual energy, yet it must
come to our consciousness through the channels of the
mind, and we should learn to co-operate intelligently
with the work of the Holy Ghost in our hearts, availing
ourselves of those little-known laws of the Inner Life
which the Church of Rome understands so well, and
which faith-healers and revivalists avail themselves of
without understanding.

Just as man consists of spirit, soul and body, so does
the Church. Her spirit is the Grace of God ; her body
is the mundane organisation ; but her soul is the spiritual
life of her children. If this be inert and perfunctory, as
it has been at certain periods of her history, the Church
is even as a man would be if the functions of his mind
were in abeyance. Spirit and body have no communica-
tion one with another, and he is an imbecile. But if the
intelligence awaken, then does the spirit within him
find expression.

God is ever more ready to give than we are to receive,
but He cannot pour the grace of His power into the
organisation of the Church save through the collective
consciousness of Her children.

EASTER EVEN

" GRANT, O Lord, that as we are baptised into the death
of thy blessed Son our Saviour Jesus Christ, so by
continual mortifying our corrupt affections we may be
buried with him ; and that through the grave, and gate
of death, we may pass to our joyful resurrection ; for
his merits, who died, and was buried, and rose again
for us, thy Son Jesus Christ our Lord. Amen."

KEYNOTE : SPIRITUAL JOY

" Through the grave, and gate of death, we pass to our
joyful resurrection," says the collect.   The place of joy
in the Christian discipline is but little understood. The
Church, realising the supreme significance of the Passion,
stresses the doctrine of purification through suffering
until suffering has become the keynote of the Christian
discipline.   This is a great half-truth which is mis-
leading. The education of the soul through suffering is
a prime law of mystic psychology, but suffering is not
the be-all and end-all of the Way of the Cross.   If we
read the story of the Passion we shall note that the Way
of the Cross begins in Gethsemane, but it does not end
on Calvary. The story of the Crucifixion terminates,
not with the burial of Our Lord, but with His glorious
Resurrection. It is the Resurrection which is the cul-
mination of the Passion, not the Death.

This wonderful prayer teaches us that it is by " mortifying our corrupt affections " that we share in Our Lord's death, and thence in His joyful Resurrection. It is the death of evil qualities that is the desired sacrifice. It is our lower self we fasten to the Cross in order that our higher self may rise into freedom with joy. We cannot manifest our true selves until the baser side of our nature has been put to the sacrificial death. Then do we rise into newness of life and spiritual freedom. Then, and then only, can we know joy. There is no joy in the gratification of the animal passions. Pleasure is not the same thing as joy. It is only when the spirit in man is free from the imperious domination of the senses that it can bring the Godhead down into manhood and take the manhood up into the Godhead.

Let us take for our meditation this week the death of all that is coarse, cowardly and selfish in our natures and the freeing of the spirit within us, so that our ideals, not our passions, shall govern our lives. Then indeed shall we have a joyful resurrection of the Christ Within.

EASTER DAY

" ALMIGHTY God, who through thine only-begotten Son Jesus Christ hast overcome death, and opened unto us the gate of everlasting life ; we humbly beseech thee, that, as by thy special grace preventing us thou dost put into our minds good desires, so by thy continual help we may bring the same to good effect ; through Jesus Christ our Lord, who liveth and reigneth with thee and the Holy Ghost, ever one God, world without end. Amen."

KEYNOTE : RESURRECTION

It was always claimed for the Greek Mysteries that their greatest gift to their initiates was freedom from the fear of death. In this collect we have the clearest possible expression of the same idea. " Almighty God, who through thine only-begotten Son Jesus Christ hast overcome death, and opened unto us the gate of ever-lasting life——" are the opening words of the collect. Can it indeed be said that the Master Jesus enables us to overcome death ? The Christian mystic knows this statement to be literally true. Christ's teaching it is which enables us to take our manhood up into Godhead through the spiritualisation of the personality by that discipline which enables human consciousness to realise Divinity. " In my flesh shall I see God " if my daily life be consecrated by the ideal of the Christ-life. The

84

little seed of good desires, the first faint stirrings of spiritual impulses will never be brought to good effect if they be buried under the unconsecrated earth of daily life. Unless the earth of everyday be made holy ground the seeds of divine impulses will not grow in it. We can only hope to overcome death if we have overcome life.

The break which death makes in the continuity of consciousness will only be overcome when consciousness can be lifted beyond the planes upon which death operates ; beyond the senses, beyond the desires, beyond even the intellect, into a realisation of spiritual existence. When we have that, then " our life is hid with Christ in God," and the second death, the death of consciousness, has no power over us.

Our Lord gives us dominion over the power of death by enabling us through His discipline so to raise consciousness that we have the realisation of eternal life here and now. " Upon such the second death has no power."

THE FIRST SUNDAY AFTER EASTER

" ALMIGHTY Father, who hast given thine only Son to die for our sins, and to rise again for our justification ; grant us so to put away the leaven of malice and wickedness, that we may alway serve thee in pureness of living and truth ; through the merits of the same thy Son Jesus Christ our Lord. Amen."

KEYNOTE : PURITY

The great sacrifice of the Crucifixion is over and the work of the Risen Christ has begun. The living Christ is with us always, " even unto the end of the world," and demands of us Christian lives. We must begin our work with Him by putting away all malice and wickedness, so that we may serve Him in pureness of living and in truth.

These two qualities, when meditated upon, yield profound truths to thought. Dirt has been defined as misplaced matter. Evil may be defined as misplaced force, and that particular aspect of evil which we call impurity is the intrusion of a primitive type of force on to a plane where it has no right to be. The instincts which we share with the animals are noble and pure upon their own plane ; it is only when they swamp the affections that they are impure. Purity of life does not mean the emasculation of the instinctive impulses, but their right use. The stress laid by the Roman Church upon celibacy has warped our concept of purity into sexlessness, but the dedication of the life-forces can be effected upon all planes. Purity does not consist in abstention from the use of our God-given instincts, but in keeping of them clean by never using them for any base purposes.

This collect also teaches us that we must serve God in truth. This is a big demand. The former requirement—that we should serve God in pureness of living—deals with our own inner lives, but the latter demand deals with our relations with the world and our fellows. If we serve God in truth we can never consent to share in the acting of a lie, or any departure from eternal verities. This will speedily bring us into collision with the world, and we shall be looked upon as fools, lacking in discretion and stirrers up of strife. But it is only by means of those souls who dare to live in truth that the law of God can be made apparent unto men. This is one of the sacrifices we are called upon to make ; this is our scourging at the hands of Pilate—that we shall live in truth before God and take the consequences at the hands of men. Not otherwise can the Kingdom be brought to earth.

THE SECOND SUNDAY AFTER EASTER

" ALMIGHTY God, who hast given thine only Son to be unto us both a sacrifice for sin, and also an ensample of godly life; give us grace that we may always most thankfully receive that his inestimable benefit, and also daily endeavour ourselves to follow the blessed steps of his most holy life; through the same Jesus Christ our Lord. Amen."

KEYNOTE: " GIVE US THY GRACE "

What do we mean when we pray for grace? Has the word any meaning for us? Grace is that energising of the spiritual nature which comes from Communion with God, from the lifting up of consciousness to listen in the Silence while the power of God pours down like invisible light till our whole nature is aglow. When we pray for strength, we receive strength, and when we pray for comfort, we receive comfort; but when we pray for grace the whole spiritual life is quickened.

If we prayed for grace instead of specific benefits, we should not find that our prayers so often had no apparent answer.

Especially is it needful to pray for God's grace when we are in temptation. When we pray to be delivered from the temptation, we are, in the very act of prayer, fixing our minds upon it. The more we think about temptation, the worse it becomes. Our surest way to resistance is to say, " Get thee behind me, Satan," and putting our problems out of our mind, pray to God for His grace and dwell upon its ways in our lives. This will give us beauty for ashes. Our minds are turned away from our obsessing temptations and are rested. Against the lure of the lower self we oppose the lure of the higher self which calls us to the beauty and light and joy of the Kingdom. As we think on these things, the calls of our lower nature lose their power ; the fear which is paralysing us is forgotten, and our thoughts are turned into new channels. God's grace has done its work.

It is the living Presence of the Christ Within which marks the difference between " Churchianity " and Christianity ; it is this which effects the transubstantiation of the elements of our nature until they cease to belong to the animal kingdom and awake to the Kingdom of God. It is this which is the Great Work of the Christ Within, the bringing up of the manhood into Godhead. It is for the sake of this achievement that the soul passes through its Gethsemane and Calvary and rises on the third day, in a body (or faculty) of spiritual realisation.

THE THIRD SUNDAY AFTER EASTER

" ALMIGHTY God, who showest to them that be in error the light of thy truth, to the intent that they may return into the way of righteousness ; grant unto all them that are admitted into the fellowship of Christ's Religion, that they may eschew those things that are contrary to their profession, and follow all such things as are agreeable to the same ; through our Lord Jesus Christ. Amen."

KEYNOTE : THE ENLIGHTENED UNDER-STANDING

This collect emphasises a very vital point in the life of the Path—the power to know right from wrong. Many people think that this is a simple enough matter, but those who have touched the deeper things of life know that this is not the case. The threads of right and wrong may be so inextricably interwoven that sometimes we cannot see how they can be disentangled without rending the fabric of life itself. Conventional maxims are a guide to expediency rather than spiritual righteousness ; the soul that is really facing life's issues has not so simple a task as the shallow generalisations of popular morality would have us believe.

Right and wrong are not always clear-cut issues. Especially is it difficult in the long-drawn-out contests of daily life to know if we are maintaining the attitude of the Mind of Christ, for it is so easy to be mislead by our own feelings and to let self-justification blind us.

Modern thinkers often tell us that it is ridiculously servile to say that without God's help we cannot hope to please God ; but, knowing what we do of human nature, is it not only too true ? How easily do we lower our ideals and blind our eyes to our failure ? We must return again and yet again to our silent communion with the Spirit of God if we are to maintain our clarity of vision. We must go apart into the Silence in order to get our bearings, otherwise we shall wander by the way.

Unless the inspiration of this silent inner contact with the Mind of God be ever with us, we shall not be able to work to the pattern shown us in the Mount. It is the Holy Spirit, directing and ruling the heart, which is our surest guide, not our reason. If God's Holy Spirit does not rule our hearts, then our instincts will rule them. We must open our hearts to the inflowing of this Divine Influence in order that our eyes may be enlightened and we may see our way clearly, otherwise we shall see nothing but the shadow thrown by our own personality.

Our greatest safeguard in these matters is humility ; a clear-sighted recognition that even our loftiest endeavours may be misplaced, our highest ideals mistaken. In facing this realisation we do not dishonour God, nor are we faithless to our ideals, rather do we honour Him by realising that His nature and plans may transcend our grasp, and that we may have imperfectly apprehended them. If we have the open mind that is willing to learn, God is willing to teach, and will not leave us comfortless, but will send to us another Comforter, to abide with us always, even the Spirit of Truth.

The Spirit of Truth can only come to those who are humble and willing to reconsider each and every position in the light of clearer understanding in so far as that shall be vouchsafed to them. To such the light grows clearer and clearer, even unto the perfect understanding of God's plan and comprehension of His nature.

For this week let us set ourselves the task of sacrificing upon the altar of Truth our self-esteem, our prestige in the eyes of men, our consistency, in order that we may invoke the Spirit of Truth to come and make His dwelling with us and enlighten our darkness. " Blessed are the poor in spirit, for theirs is the Kingdom of God."

THE FOURTH SUNDAY AFTER EASTER

" O ALMIGHTY God, who alone canst order the unruly wills and affections of sinful men ; grant unto thy people, that they may love the thing which thou commandest, and desire that which thou dost promise ; that so, among the sundry and manifold changes of the world, our hearts may surely there be fixed, where true joys are to be found ; through Jesus Christ our Lord. Amen."

KEYNOTE : THE JOY OF THE SPIRIT

There is a deep psychology contained in this collect, for its writer realises that the compulsion of the will overruling the desires does not give a true spiritual state, but rather produces a house divided against itself, which cannot long stand securely. Very wisely we are taught to pray that we may love the things which God commands and desire that which He promises, because this love and desire rightly fixed, will bring us to the state where true joys are to be found. The tenor of this collect emphasises the fact that true spirituality, although it comes to birth through travail and the pangs of the soul, is fundamentally joyous and spontaneous when it has reached its full stature. The saints are those who have overcome. Saintship is not repression of evil desires or a denial of the appetites of the lower self, but a spiritualisation of the entire nature till the whole man is fit to meet God face to face. This should be our aim, to bring the Godhead down into manhood, and thereby take the manhood up into Godhead, not to divide the spirit and soul asunder.

Let us accept the inevitability of God's will and the absolute rightness of His law, for, as Saint Thomas Aquinas so truly said, " A thing is not just because God wills it, but God wills it because it is just." Not otherwise can we find peace and harmony, for our harmony is entirely dependent upon our adjustment to the laws of the Cosmos. Let us accept and adjust, and then we shall be at peace. Let us meditate upon the unity of all manifested existence and our own relation to it, then shall we desire to be in harmony with that of which we are an integral part, and this desire, steadily followed, will bring us to the state where true joys are to be found.

THE FIFTH SUNDAY AFTER EASTER

" O LORD, from whom all good things do come ; grant
to us thy humble servants, that by thy holy inspiration
we may think those things that be good, and by thy
merciful guiding may perform the same ; through our
Lord Jesus Christ. Amen."

KEYNOTE : GOD'S GUIDANCE

This is a prayer of exquisite simplicity which all who
seek enlightenment through the intellect and who are
strong in their own strength would do well to make
their own. We are all too apt, when things are going
well with us, to think that the circle of our vision circum-
scribes the universe, that beyond the horizon there are
no forces at work which may overset our plans ; but
the Fathers of the Church, men wise in human nature
as well as in spiritual doctrine, knew otherwise, and so
we get this exquisite gem of the child-heart, this little
prayer for help and guidance to do simple things rightly,
the things that look so easy and obvious, and yet which
are the acid-tests of the attitude of the soul. If our natural
attitude of mind were truly expressed by this prayer,
how many errors it would save us from, how much
suffering it would guard us from ! This should be the
daily prayer of the intellectual and strong-willed, for its
sweet sanity and deep wisdom are what we need to

preserve our souls from contamination from within, where is to be found the most subtle source of spiritual poison.

This week, therefore, let us not only pray this wonderful prayer, but pray that we may pray it aright, that its significance may sink into our souls and guard them from spiritual darkness and the falls that come therefrom, and that its profound teaching may penetrate the limitations of our intellect and enlighten us with the wisdom of the spirit which transcends knowledge and enlightens the judgment that is according to reason.

THE ASCENSION DAY

" GRANT, we beseech thee, Almighty God, that like as we do believe thy only-begotten Son our Lord Jesus Christ to have ascended into the heavens ; so we may also in heart and mind thither ascend, and with him continually dwell, who liveth and reigneth with thee and the Holy Ghost, one God, world without end. Amen."

KEYNOTE : THE VISION BEAUTIFUL

This collect contains a profound doctrine concerning the nature of the enlightenment which comes to souls in search of spiritual illumination. Our Lord no longer walks and talks with us as He did with the people of His day in Galilee ; He has ascended to the right hand of God, and there functions as a great force in the cosmic polity. If we think we are directly taught of Him as a child of its tutor, we err in our vanity. It may well be possible for the greatest of human souls, in supreme moments, to so rise up and contact Him ; but those of us, aspirants after the Way of the Cross, to whom is vouchsafed the wonderful vision of Our Lord, are not meeting Him face to face, but are, in reality, contacting His force and translating it through the imagination as a meeting with His personality.

Let us not flatter ourselves with vanities. The things of God are greater than psychic phenomena, and this collect gives us a truer interpretation of our experiences. It is the Holy Ghost, the Spirit of Truth that abides with us and never leaves us comfortless, and that at last brings us to the state of consciousness where we can meet the Master face to face, that is to say, where we can comprehend Him, and know even as we are known.

Let us take for our discipline this week the task of rising above the concepts that help the young soul to lay hold on the things of the Kingdom, and, foregoing the milk of the word which is for babes, try to assimilate those spiritual verities which, though a hard doctrine, are the strong meat on which souls which have reached their manhood in the spiritual life are enabled to run the race that is set before them. The still small voice of realisation, brought through to consciousness by discipline, purification, and sacrifice, can teach us more of the innermost nature of things than any spectacular psychic experience. Let us never forget that the big things are simple and natural, and be content with wholesome spiritual food rather than seek in exotic cults and abnormal manifestations the satisfaction of a depraved spiritual appetite, which seeks after marvels and sees not the Master sitting quietly at the well-head of Truth whence the village women have always drawn their water.

THE SUNDAY AFTER ASCENSION DAY

" O GOD the King of Glory, who hast exalted thine only Son Jesus Christ with great triumph unto thy kingdom in heaven ; we beseech thee, leave us not comfortless but send to us thine Holy Ghost to comfort us, and exalt us unto the same place whither our Saviour Christ is gone before, who liveth and reigneth with thee and the Holy Ghost, one God, world without end. Amen."

KEYNOTE : INVOCATION OF THE HOLY GHOST

This collect is an invocation of the Holy Ghost Whose coming shall raise us to Christ-consciousness. What then is it that we invoke thus, and what shall Christ-consciousness be when we have attained it ?

The Holy Ghost is that aspect of the Godhead Whose functioning relates to the things of the mind. God the Father is the Creator and Sustainer of all that is ; God the Son is the Redeemer, the Teacher of the Heart, the Lord of Love and Compassion ; but God the Holy Ghost is the Illuminator of the Mind, Who shall bring all things to our remembrance and give us understanding of the deep things, yea, even of the hidden things of God.

We know little in modern Christianity concerning the nature and office of the Holy Ghost, yet herein lie the deeper aspects of our faith. It is the Holy Ghost Who is the Initiator of the Christian into the Mysteries of Jesus— that deeper understanding of the divine doctrine which was given to the disciples when Our Lord took them apart and taught them in the upper chamber and which gave them powers that enabled them to say to their Master, " Even the devils are subject unto us through Thy Name."

Just as through the work of the Son we find healing for sin and sorrow, so through the work of the Holy Ghost we find understanding and illumination. We should not be content, therefore, only to call upon Our Lord to seek and save that which is lost, but we should also pray for God's Holy Spirit to come upon us and open our eyes to the vision of the Kingdom and our understanding to the deep things of the Spirit.

Then shall we be exalted into the same place whither our Saviour Christ is gone, for we shall have that mind in us which was also in Christ Jesus, and shall know even as we are known.

WHIT SUNDAY

" GOD, who as at this time didst teach the hearts of thy faithful people, by the sending to them the light of thy Holy Spirit ; grant us by the same Spirit to have a right judgment in all things, and evermore to rejoice in his holy comfort ; through the merits of Christ Jesus our Saviour, who liveth and reigneth with thee, in the unity of the same Spirit, one God, world without end. Amen."

KEYNOTE : THE PERCEPTION OF THE CHRIST

The discipline of the Master Jesus brings us to the living contact of the Holy Ghost. When our personalities have been purified by this discipline, the light of spiritual understanding illuminates our consciousness. If we have done rightly the work demanded of us throughout the period of purgation, if we have shared in our Master's passion and resurrection, then, at Whitsuntide when the great Power-tides descend upon the world, we shall receive of the spiritual forces according to our utmost need and capacity. It is for us to prepare our hearts for the indwelling of the Holy Spirit ; to make them clean and ready ; to watch at the door for the first glimpse of the Divine Visitant, for it is only to the prepared consciousness that the Guest comes.

Let us do the best we know and await with eagerness

and confidence the Coming in the Heart of the Whitsuntide Power, and we shall not be disappointed.

Often, however, a test heralds the Coming, as the old
stories so often tell; we have to recognise the Divine
Visitant in strange guises. The beggar asks us for alms ;
we give what we can, and lo, he sheds his ragged cloak
and there is the Prince of Peace ! The Christ always
comes as the Man of Sorrows, never as the heralded
Messiah. We must be faithful over few things before
we are made ruler of many. As the collect so truly says,
it is to the " faithful people " that the teaching of the
Spirit is given, not to the gifted. The Master values
fidelity more highly than great gifts.

Let us, therefore, at the great Power-season of
Whitsuntide listen mentally for the still small voice of
the Comforter to speak in our hearts. Let us make
ourselves receptive, knowing that the power of the Holy
Ghost is pouring through in strong tides upon the earth.
According to our faith will it be unto us.

TRINITY SUNDAY

" ALMIGHTY and everlasting God, who hast given unto
us thy servants grace by the confession of a true faith to
acknowledge the glory of the eternal Trinity, and in the
power of the Divine Majesty to worship the Unity ; we
beseech thee that thou wouldest keep us stedfast in this
faith, and evermore defend us from all adversities, who
livest and reignest, one God, world without end. Amen."

KEYNOTE : MYSTICAL UNDERSTANDING

The collect for this Sunday, together with the Epistle
and Gospel, are so profoundly metaphysical in their
significance that at first sight they would appear to be
mere words idly strung together. To those, however,
who understand the connotation of the symbolism
employed, this is far from being the case. Every word
in the profoundly mystical passages chosen for this day
has its significance, and the collect itself prays that understanding may be given us to penetrate this significance.

The wording of the collect is very pregnant. We are
told that " by the confession of a true faith " we are able
to " acknowledge the glory of the eternal Trinity, and in
the power of the Divine Majesty to worship the Unity."

Faith we may define as an opinion which is based on
intuition rather than upon logical grounds. It is by
intuition, not reason, that we gain a realisation of the

supreme mystery of manifestation, the triune nature and functioning of the Logos.   But this intuitive realisation being gained, we are not left dependent upon blind faith, but " in the power of the Divine Majesty " are able " to worship the Unity."

What is this " power of the Divine Majesty " which is thus conveyed to us ?   The collect does not specify, but should we be beyond the range of legitimate speculation if we held that it was the Christ Within ?

The spirit of man, enabled to function by a faith which dares to trust, and to experiment with an open mind in the things of the Spirit, is not left long without evidence in support of what was originally a working hypothesis ; the wakened Christ Within is able to worship, to establish contact with the Unity—with the Great Unmanifest, the source of all existence, the inexhaustible fountain-head of power, and this realisation enables us to overcome in the Name of God all opposition when about our Father's business.

THE FIRST SUNDAY AFTER TRINITY

" O GOD, the strength of all them that put their trust
in thee, mercifully accept our prayers ; and because
through the weakness of our mortal nature we can do no
good thing without thee, grant us the help of thy grace,
that in keeping of thy commandments we may please
thee, both in will and deed ; through Jesus Christ our
Lord. Amen."

KEYNOTE : " THE WEAPONS OF OUR WARFARE ARE NOT CARNAL "

Again and again the collects teach us to rely upon
God and not upon our own strength. This is not a
confession of weakness nor the resort of feeble natures,
but means that when we are dedicated to the service of
our Master, " the weapons of our warfare are not carnal."
It does not mean that we cease to struggle and become
supine, but that the scene of our struggles has shifted
from the outer to the inner planes. Those who understand the significance of the Inner Life keep still upon
the mundane plane when great events are toward, for
they know that the mundane plane is only the plane of
effects, and that all causation is in the unseen. Their
struggle, therefore, is not with principalities and powers
but with themselves, as they endeavour to obtain a clear
realisation of the power of God, and to hold that realisa-

tion steadily in spite of the evidence of the senses, so that the thought-form so made may act as a channel for the Divine Force to come through into the plane of form.

Let us, therefore, meditate on the omnipotent, all-wise and all-loving Logos and then invoke the Logoidal power to manifest through us for the working out of the Cosmic Law, and we shall find that all the problems which are presented to us in the Master's service will solve themselves.

THE SECOND SUNDAY AFTER TRINITY

" O LORD, who never failest to help and govern them whom thou dost bring up in thy stedfast fear and love ; keep us, we beseech thee, under the protection of thy good providence, and make us to have a perpetual fear and love of thy holy Name ; through Jesus Christ our Lord. Amen."

KEYNOTE : THE GOOD LAW

When we are beset with the difficulties of daily life, when its tragedies overshadow us, we ask ourselves whether there is indeed a Divine law ordering all things, and, if there be such a law, is it responsible for all the misery and useless suffering we see about us.

One thing is self-evident—if no law ordered the universe it must long ago have shaken itself to pieces from sheer friction. Why should we conclude that natural law stops short with the lower animals ?

When we come to consider man, with his intelligence and a will sufficiently free to be a determining factor in his fate, we have to expand our conception of natural law to include those higher aspects of his nature, latent in many, subconscious in most, but conscious in a few, which, for lack of a better term, we call spiritual. Surely the spiritual aspect of man's nature is just as natural as the emotional. It is neither a pathology nor a miracle, but a higher stage of evolution. It may be having a hard struggle for survival in the present age, but nevertheless, we can see that it is going to inherit the earth in due course of evolutionary time.

May we not believe that there are natural laws of the spiritual plane of existence which govern this aspect of man's nature, and are vital, though disregarded factors in the polity of nations, which, when broken, are responsible for the mass of human misery we see about us, just as the laws of hygiene, when broken, are to us the administrators of disease ? Should we attribute to Divine Wrath the results of man's ignorant wilfulness ? Can we plead ignorance as an excuse after God has given us a standard of manhood in Christ Jesus Our Lord ? We all know better than we do. It is the cumulative effect of human shortcomings that piles up the sum of human misery.

If every single human being were pure, and diligent in his Father's business, and compassionate, the world's misery would be wiped out in one generation. For think what it would mean : sensuality would no longer bring into the world weakly bodies and depraved minds, and spread the racial poisons ; selfishness would no longer ignore human needs and cause the poverty diseases ; self-indulgence and sloth would no longer produce their inevitable results. Death would come to us in the calm sleep of old age or the swift extinction of accident, even as it comes to the animal kingdom under natural law.

We must keep God's law, not cry out against it ; and being our brother's keeper, must suffer with him when all creation groaneth and travaileth together. But if in all our ways we love God's law and fear to break it, then will He never fail to help and govern us ; and the first earnest of the fulfilling of His law will be the inner peace that comes to us, even amidst the human confusion that still overspreads the earth.

THE THIRD SUNDAY AFTER TRINITY

" O LORD, we beseech thee mercifully to hear us ; and grant that we, to whom thou hast given an hearty desire to pray, may by thy mighty aid be defended and comforted in all dangers and adversities ; through Jesus Christ our Lord. Amen."

KEYNOTE : THE POWER OF PRAYER

Those who follow an intellectual way to God are all too apt to fail to avail themselves of the power of prayer. The positive character loves to go in its own might, and seeks rather to increase its strength and understanding than to rely upon any external aid. The beginning of wisdom is to know our own limitations. We are not sufficient unto ourselves save in times of peace. The collect, with wise insight, reminds us that we are not only defended by God's aid, but comforted. Even when our strength can manage to maintain a brave outer show, even when it has been able to carry all before it success-fully, who has not known the need for inner comfort in the hour of anxiety before the dawn or when the cost is counted after the victory ?

Let us, therefore, while our souls are at peace, learn the power of prayer, so that, when our strength becomes weakness and our judgment is darkened in the hour of trial, we may be able to reach out beyond ourselves and lay hold upon God's strength and wisdom.

Prayer lifts the soul to the heights. There, raised above its perplexities, it wins to clear vision. The power of God flows in upon it, and it renews its strength ; the peace of God soothes it and the protection of God gives it rest. Lifted by prayer to the contemplation of the eternal verities, we measure our problems against them and gain a sense of proportion. Drawn back to God by prayer, we become once again as children, and our Father is Love.

THE FOURTH SUNDAY AFTER TRINITY

" O GOD, the protector of all that trust in thee, without whom nothing is strong, nothing is holy ; increase and multiply upon us thy mercy ; that, thou being our ruler and guide, we may so pass through things temporal, that we finally lose not the things eternal ; grant this, O heavenly Father, for Jesus Christ's sake our Lord. Amen."

KEYNOTE : THE TWO STANDPOINTS

There are two standpoints from which we can look at life. The standpoint of the lower self, with its background of the senses ; and the standpoint of the higher self, with its background of Spirit. The higher self is developed and awakened by means of the experiences which fall to the lot of the lower self in its struggles with life in the flesh. When the struggle is painful and unavailing, when the denial of the pleasures of the senses and the gratification of human desires forces us to seek a higher aid, when the barrenness of external things forces us to look within, we are in little danger of becoming enmeshed in matter. But when the lower self is on a flowing tide of prosperity, or when it is spurred by a fear for the loss of its accustomed flesh-pots, we are all too apt to live exclusively in things temporal and lose sight of the eternal values by which the soul's account must ultimately be balanced.

Even more in prosperity than in loss do we need the contact of spiritual forces, or, to use the old phraseology, the blessing of God, to rest upon our lives, lest we forget the purpose of life, which is the evolution of the soul, not the gratification of the senses. Let us measure all things against a background of infinity, and life itself will become for us the Way of Enlightenment.

THE FIFTH SUNDAY AFTER TRINITY

" GRANT, O Lord, we beseech thee, that the course of this world may be so peaceably ordered by thy governance, that thy Church may joyfully serve thee in all godly quietness ; through Jesus Christ our Lord. Amen."

KEYNOTE : " THY KINGDOM COME "

The true lover of God desires to see the coming of the Kingdom on earth among men. The prayer, " Thy Kingdom come " is not an idle form of words for him. Do all of us, who repeat these words mechanically as part of the Lord's Prayer, realise their significance in relation to the world's affairs ? The next words of the prayer give us the clue—" Thy will be done, on earth as it is in heaven."

God's will is the Cosmic Law, and the Cosmic Law is not an arbitrary enactment, but the expression of God's nature. That nature was shown forth to us in the life of Christ Jesus. There, then, we have our model. God's will is done when we live Christ-like lives. If everybody did this, His Kingdom would come on earth as it is in heaven. The kingdom of heaven is not a place, nor yet a form of government, but the state of consciousness which has become habituated to the Christ-ideal and dwells constantly in it.

The kingdom comes first in our own hearts ; and in

so far as we realise its nature we can bring it into being in the world of men in spite of all difficulty and opposition by consistently and determinedly bringing each one of our actions into line with that ideal.

It is only through a change of individual consciousness that the kingdom of heaven will come on earth. No form of government can bring it, because it is the outward and visible sign of an inward and spiritual grace. It proceeds spontaneously from an attitude of mind and state of feeling ; it cannot be enforced from without by laws and magistrates. Outward force may produce civil order, but it can never produce " peace and joy and godly quietness," and these are the signs by which we know that " the Lord keepeth the city."

THE SIXTH SUNDAY AFTER TRINITY

" O GOD, who hast prepared for them that love thee such good things as pass man's understanding ; pour into our hearts such love towards thee, that we, loving thee above all things, may obtain thy promises, which exceed all that we can desire ; through Jesus Christ our Lord. Amen."

KEYNOTE : THE LOVE OF GOD

The Outer Church teaches the power of the love of God towards us, but the Hidden Church teaches the power of our love for God.

Little do we realise the tremendous potency of the yearning of the soul for the Divine Reality. When the whole soul goes forth seeking God out of an instinctive longing for the Bread of Life, it contacts the things of the Spirit at a far higher level than when it cries out for God's love to comfort it or His power to save it from its enemies.

When we seek to know God by the power of the understanding, we can rise no higher than a knowledge of the manner in which the Divine Light shines through the prism of forms. The understanding is of value to us after we have known God as He is, but not before ; such studies will not take us to God ; in fact, if we have no realisation of the true nature of that which we seek, they may darken our vision by holding the mind fast to the bondage of form.

The knowledge of God begins when the operations of the mind end. It is by a form of consciousness which transcends thought that we apprehend spiritual realities. There is but one thing which will draw the soul across the great gulf which is fixed between matter and spirit, and that is an outgoing of strong love towards That which is on the farther side of the gulf.

Then, as we so love, in silence and in stillness, asking nothing of the Love of God save that we may love more and more, the Whisper from the Silence comes across the great gulf, for consciousness has " tuned in " to the keynote of God.

THE SEVENTH SUNDAY AFTER TRINITY

" LORD of all power and might, who art the author and giver of all good things ; graft in our hearts the love of thy Name, increase in us true religion, nourish us with all goodness, and of thy great mercy keep us in the same ; through Jesus Christ our Lord. Amen."

KEYNOTE : THE POWER OF GOD

There are many different aspects under which God can be worshipped, aspects corresponding to the different forms of the Divine Essence in manifestation, for we know God only in His functions. We may adore God as Love, or worship Him as Wisdom, but there is another aspect that is sometimes forgotten in these days of a refined culture which abhors pain—the aspect of God as Power.

It is because this is so often forgotten that religion is apt to be " feeble, mawkish, and unmanly ". It is only when the Power aspect re-enforces the Wisdom and the Love that the great chord of God is struck, the chord that can overthrow the walls of all the fortified cities of materialism.

We must train ourselves to reverence the great sweeping Power aspect of God, but not to fear it. We have no need to fear it so long as we keep God's law. If we dare to trust ourselves to its tremendous current, we open a channel whereby it can flow through us into the world. But that channel, once opened, cannot be closed by our hands. There must be no faltering or turning back if we push out from the shore and give ourselves to be borne along by the rushing river of the Power of God. That way lies destruction; for the great forces we have invoked, though pure as fire, will shatter the frail bark of our wilfulness if we turn it against the stream of their force. We can only touch the great things of life if we dare to invoke the Power of God to come upon us.

But the Wisdom and the Love come equally with the Power, and so we have no need to fear anything save our own weaknesses and impurity. If the Power of God came alone, it would overwhelm us, but if by our lives, we have brought into manifestation first the Love and then the Wisdom of God, we may safely invoke the Power, though not otherwise. Power, following upon Love and Wisdom, renders them potent. Without that Power, they are negative, inert. Love may will and Wisdom may design, but it is the Power of God which is " the author and giver of all good things."

THE EIGHTH SUNDAY AFTER TRINITY

" O GOD, whose never-failing providence ordereth all things both in heaven and earth ; we humbly beseech thee to put away from us all hurtful things, and to give us those things which be profitable for us ; through Jesus Christ our Lord. Amen."

KEYNOTE : THE CHOICE OF THE SOUL

Desire is prayer. When we desire a thing, we are invoking it as far as lies in our power, and a great deal more lies in our power than we realise, though its manifestations are not always seen in the immediate future.

How many souls would dare to pray, " Put away from us all hurtful things and give us those things which be profitable for us," if they thought that their prayer was going to have an immediate answer ! Is not our prayer all too often, " O Lord, save us from the consequences of our actions and make the things we like profitable for us——"

How many souls are prepared to found their house of life on the rock of truth ? How many try to drive piles into the shifting sands of phantasy and evasion in order to secure a firm foundation ? Such a pile-driving is an expensive process, and a house erected on insecure foundations is an insecure dwelling at the best of times, and in constant need of repair.

We shall never know security, or freedom, or happiness, or health until we determine that our lives shall be founded upon truth in their every aspect, and that we will fearlessly and without counting the cost, " turn and overturn, till He whose right it is shall reign," for whatever the cost may be, it is less than the price of keeping a house built upon sand in a state of repair.

If we could only dare to pray that great prayer in sincerity how different our lives would be, and how much more we should have to show for them at the final accounting. If we are willing to part with whatever is hurtful to us, however sweet it be, and to welcome whatever is profitable to us, however hard it be, our house of life will be of sound workmanship, founded on the rock, and will stand fast in the day of tempest, sheltering us and our loved ones in security when " the blast of the terrible ones is as a storm against the wall."

The higher life can only be lived in proportion to our courage, honesty, and staying-power. Even though there be vision, the people will perish without this holy but humble trinity, for they are the hidden foundations of the higher life.

THE NINTH SUNDAY AFTER TRINITY

" GRANT to us, Lord, we beseech thee, the spirit to think and do always such things as be rightful ; that we, who cannot do anything that is good without thee, may by thee be enabled to live according to thy will ; through Jesus Christ our Lord. Amen."

KEYNOTE : RIGHT UNDERSTANDING

Life seldom presents to us a clear-cut issue, and it is not always easy to know what is the right thing to do. We may earnestly desire to do the right thing, and yet, by an error of judgment, do untold harm. Again, our own subconscious desires may mislead us until we " rationalise " our actions so that our judgment concerning right and wrong fits in with our desires.

How are we to know what is " God's will "—the spiritual principle which governs the situation ? Only by putting aside all personal feelings in the matter, and attuning ourselves to the Spirit of God.

In order to do this, let us first read awhile in the inspired Writings of those who themselves were in tune with God. Their outlook will guide us and their spirit will influence us. By their companionship and counsel our hearts will insensibly be brought into that spirit which is in tune with God and we shall " judge righteous judgment."

Then, laying on the altar all our personal desires and prejudices in order that at whatever cost we shall do the right thing, we may pray to God to " Grant us the spirit to think and to do always such things as be rightful ; that we may be enabled to live according to thy will." Then if we have " kept back no part of the price " we shall find the Wisdom of God speaking in the still small voice of the higher self and our path will become clear and our souls will be at peace.

THE TENTH SUNDAY AFTER TRINITY

" LET thy merciful ears, O Lord, be open to the prayers of thy humble servants ; and that they may obtain their petitions make them to ask such things as shall please thee ; through Jesus Christ our Lord. Amen."

KEYNOTE : RIGHT PRAYING

Prayer is a very great power, and it is but very little understood. God does not give us things because we ask for them, and withhold them because we do not ask for them. The Divine Life forever flows forth as from an unfailing spring, and we live and move and have our being within it as fish swim in the waters of the ocean. It is not God's giving which fails, but our receiving.

What do we seek in prayer ? The gratification of our desires ? We ask our Divine Father for that which we want just as unthinkingly as children ask for a penny. But we have been given minds with which to think and wills with which to act ; we are no longer children and must put away childish things when we approach our Divine Father with petitions.

If the child, grown to manhood, goes to his father and asks for pounds instead of pennies to spend on idle pleasures, will he get them ? No. But if he asks for the means to an honourable career, will not his father strain every effort to give it to him ?

So it is when we approach God with our prayers. Do we ask things worthy of spiritual adults ? Do we ask to be relieved from suffering, to be spared the fulfilment of our fears, to be saved from the consequences of our errors ? If so, we ask amiss. We are children asking for pennies. But do we ask for courage and understanding, love and patience, and God's light to illumine our darkness, God's love to comfort our sorrow ? Then we ask as souls grown to spiritual manhood, and we shall not be denied.

THE ELEVENTH SUNDAY AFTER TRINITY

" O GOD, who declarest thy almighty power most chiefly in showing mercy and pity ; mercifully grant unto us such a measure of thy grace, that we, running the way of thy commandments, may obtain thy gracious promises, and be made partakers of thy heavenly treasure ; through Jesus Christ our Lord. Amen."

KEYNOTE :
ATTAINMENT THROUGH OBEDIENCE

God's commandments are not the arbitrary orders of a despot, any more than natural laws are the arbitrary commands of scientists. Men who understood nature have told us the result of innumerable observations and experiments expressed in a few words as formulæ, and these formulæ are called natural laws. But it is not these laws which determine the workings of nature ; nature worked long before there were scientists to observe her. It is nature which determines the laws, not the laws which determine nature.

So it is with spiritual laws, sometimes, according to the personalising habit of thought of the ancients, spoken of as God's commands. Men who knew the nature of God have told us things concerning His nature, and have formulated the Divine Principles as God's laws.

It is God's nature which determines the nature of His Universe. As God is in spirit, so is His manifestation in form. As above, so below; the Divine Nature is expressed in all that He created and sustains.

It was Christ Jesus who " showed us the Father." If " That mind be in you which was also in Christ Jesus," you will obey the commandments of God spontaneously because it is your nature to ; and just as you will be healthy if you live according to " the laws of nature," so will you be harmonious if you live according to " God's commandments " and will be " made partakers of the heavenly treasure."

THE TWELFTH SUNDAY AFTER TRINITY

" ALMIGHTY and everlasting God, who art always more ready to hear than we to pray, and art wont to give more than either we desire or deserve ; pour down upon us the abundance of thy mercy ; forgiving us those things whereof our conscience is afraid, and giving us those good things which we are not worthy to ask, but through the merits and mediation of Jesus Christ, thy Son, our Lord. Amen."

KEYNOTE : BEYOND OUR GRASP

If our aspirations were limited by our apprehensions we should be " of all men most miserable," but our hearts reach out beyond our minds, and God hears the unspoken desire and answers it.

Our lower selves, clinging desperately to their material security and their personal desires, are not able to formulate the bold and noble prayers that call down the power of God. It is our higher selves, silent and hidden in the deepest recesses of our nature, which pray for spiritual things and are answered, often to the confusion and distress of the lower self.

And all the time the Life and the Love and the Might and the Wisdom of the Logoidal Consciousness are around us like the air we breathe, pressing for admission to our self-limited natures, and we are afraid to open ourselves to them lest our small securities be swept away in the great tides of Cosmic Life.

Then it is that the higher self rises up and prays, " Give us more than we dare to ask." We open ourselves freely to the great tides of spirit, come what may. And God " who is ever more ready to hear than we are to pray," pours down upon us " more than we can ask or think," and the problems, which appeared insuperable to our darkened eyes, are swept away in the great rushing tides of Life and Love, and the memory of them is not even kept in mind.

Let us, therefore, dare to trust ourselves into God's hands, for He is indeed the Creator and Sustainer of life, and will not suffer us to be lost, but bring us, by His mercy, into the fullness of life.

THE THIRTEENTH SUNDAY AFTER TRINITY

" ALMIGHTY and merciful God, of whose only gift it cometh that thy faithful people do unto thee true and laudable service ; grant, we beseech thee, that we may so faithfully serve thee in this life, that we fail not finally to attain thy heavenly promises ; through the merits of Jesus Christ our Lord. Amen."

KEYNOTE : FIDELITY AND UNDERSTANDING

Two things are needed for God's service : one is an unfaltering fidelity, and the other is a right understanding of what is required of us.

If we look back through history, we see many examples of an unfaltering fidelity to God's service which to us seem to go hand in hand with a misunderstanding of God's requirements of us. We cannot now believe that God would require us to massacre the little children of those who believed wrongly, yet men have been found, not once but many times, to do this in a spirit of unfaltering fidelity.

How are we to avoid making like errors ? How are we to judge righteous judgment ? We cannot do it by the light of human reason and expediency ; we must be able to stand outside our mundane problems if we are to see in them their spiritual significance and judge them accordingly.

It is only by God's grace that we can hope to do this. And what is that grace ? It is the uplifting of heart that comes when we lift up our eyes to the highest ideal we can conceive—the life of Jesus of Nazareth. He is the Friend of the Heart Whose influence changes our outlook. When we have been alone with Him for a little while, we find that we are judging very differently to the way we judged when we were in the midst of our problems. Guided by the Divine Counsellor, we shall know how to do God true and laudable service, and shall not be misled by our human errors, fears, and prejudices.

THE FOURTEENTH SUNDAY AFTER TRINITY

" ALMIGHTY and everlasting God, give unto us the increase of faith, hope, and charity ; and, that we may obtain that which thou dost promise, make us to love that which dost command ; through Jesus Christ our Lord. Amen."

KEYNOTE : THE LOVE OF GOD'S LAW

It is not enough that we should obey God's law from fear of the consequences of disobedience. Unless we realise the beauty of its harmony we do not obey it with the inward man. Only when we realise that God's law is the music of the spheres, that it sweetly ruleth and governeth all things, bringing forth Mazzaroth in his season and guiding Arcturus with his sons,—only when we realise that harmony is its basis and perfection its design can we joyfully give ourselves up with perfect security to its governing. Then do we know why the morning stars sang together and all the sons of God shouted for joy.

It is our finite separateness and selfishness which keeps us from this realisation. Because we wish to keep back part of the price, to retain something for our private use, we fear to leap into the ocean of the Cosmic Life where we can swim freely and where there is an abundant sufficiency for all our needs.

It is only as we develop the vision of the higher self— the faith which perceiveth the substance of things unseen, the hope which in confidence awaits the manifestation of the hidden laws, and the love which faileth not and is kind to all things, which seeketh not its own, and therefore possesseth all things—that we can rise into realisation of the oneness of all existence and love God's law because it maintaineth infinite unity in eternal harmony.

THE FIFTEENTH SUNDAY AFTER TRINITY

" KEEP, we beseech thee, O Lord, thy Church with thy perpetual mercy; and, because the frailty of man without thee cannot but fall, keep us ever by thy help from all things hurtful, and lead us to all things profitable to our salvation; through Jesus Christ our Lord. Amen."

KEYNOTE: DIVINE GUIDANCE

Unless God keepeth the city, the watchman waketh in vain. Like water, human consciousness forever seeks its own level. It can never transcend its limitations or rise above its imperfections. It is only the pressure of Divine Life which can bring human life to higher levels.

We will infallibly be self-deluded unless we have an external standard of rightness. We will unconsciously justify that which we desire and condone that into which we have lapsed. Our judgment of ourselves soon becomes vitiated if we have no Exemplar by which to measure ourselves.

Man can no more rise higher than himself than water can rise higher than its source. It is only when we make contact with the Divine that we are lifted above the endless circle of the human. God's love, manifested to us by His Son and His Saints, shows us the way out of this vicious circle ; in humility we open our hearts to that ever-flowing love, and it pours into us with newness of life and we rise up out of our finite human concepts to the heights whence Love comes.

God's Love is an active, not a passive thing. It is the Great Reconciler. Jesus Christ was the expression of that Love, and ever it goes forth, like a shepherd seeking that which is lost. It presses into human consciousness wherever the door stands ajar. None who hunger and thirst after righteousness need go empty away. If we allow the human qualities of kindliness and gentleness to find expression through us, they will open the door to Divine Love, and Our Lord will come in and sup with us.

THE SIXTEENTH SUNDAY AFTER TRINITY

" O LORD, we beseech thee, let thy continual pity cleanse and defend thy Church ; and, because it cannot continue in safety without thy succour, preserve it evermore by thy help and goodness ; through Jesus Christ our Lord. Amen."

KEYNOTE :
" CLEANSE AND DEFEND THY CHURCH "

This collect is a prayer for the helping of the Church, and it indicates clearly in what manner that help must be sought. The Church must be " cleansed and defended," and in the wording of the collect we see that the cleansing must precede the defending. It is the enemies within our gates that are to be feared, not the enemies without, and those enemies are not persons, but conditions.

If the Church were as perfect as her Lord, she could safely " answer not a word " to her attackers. The cleansing of the Church is her best defence from her enemies. By heart-searching let her rid herself of her vulnerable points.

The collect goes on to remind us that the Church cannot continue without God's succour. Unless the power of God uses the Church as its channel of manifestation, the Church has no reason for existence, and her buildings would be as the temples of Greece from whose altars the gods have departed. Do not, however, let us make the mistake of thinking that the Church is its organisation, its parishes and bishoprics ; it does not have its habitation upon the physical plane, but is builded not with hands, eternal in the heavens. The Church is the company of souls, living, unborn, or born into the life beyond the grave, who acknowledge its discipline. It is through these that the power of God works, not through the mundane organisation, necessary as that is. An oak-wood is composed of oak-trees, and a living Church is composed of living souls. If we want to defend the Church from her enemies, let us purify our own souls and lift them up to God that His power may be seen in us and draw all men unto us.

THE SEVENTEENTH SUNDAY AFTER TRINITY

" LORD, we pray thee that thy grace may always prevent and follow us, and make us continually to be given to all good works ; through Jesus Christ our Lord. Amen."

KEYNOTE : THE GRACE OF GOD

When the grace of God illumines the soul, the whole life shines with an inner light. What do we mean by " the Grace of God " ? It means that we are consciously in touch with God, that we live our lives in His presence. We shall never understand this statement, however, if we think of God as a person in the sense in which we apply the word personality to ourselves. We may be said to be in the presence of God when consciousness apprehends some aspect of the Divine Nature, and when our characters show forth the God-qualities.

But how can we know what those God-qualities are when the Personality of God is admittedly inapprehensible by the unaided human faculties ? " No man has seen the Father at any time," but " whosoever has seen Me, has seen the Father," said Our Lord, for He showed forth in their fullest human manifestation the God-qualities. It is, therefore, " through Jesus Christ Our Lord " that we purify and uplift our natures till they meet the Grace of God ; and when the Grace of God is with them, they flow out as spontaneously in good works as the sun gives light.

How different is the quality of the " good works " thus engendered ! The God-qualities flowing through us to our fellow-men are life-giving, regenerating, for we are showing them God in our small way, even as Our Lord " showed us the Father." We are showing them God when we are loving, for God is Love ; we are showing them God when we are true, for God is Truth, the Light in Whom there is no darkness. Human souls can only know God when He is thus shown to them by the manifesting of the God-qualities in human lives. It is this which distinguishes the good works done in the Name of God ; the God-qualities we have developed in our own nature are channels for the power of God to manifest itself to men, and good works undertaken under such a Divine impulse operate upon more planes than one, and when we feed the hungry because God loves His children through us, we feed not only the body, but the immortal spirit.

THE EIGHTEENTH SUNDAY AFTER TRINITY

"LORD, we beseech thee, grant thy people grace to withstand the temptations of the world, the flesh and the devil, and with pure hearts and minds to follow thee the only God; through Jesus Christ our Lord. Amen."

KEYNOTE: THE SAVING POWER OF GRACE

Anyone who has had to struggle, whether in himself or in others, with the power of the three great instincts gone astray, knows the difficulty of finding any force to oppose the downward drag of the animal nature that is reverting to type. The only argument that is of any avail is to plead the danger of the course and appeal to the instinct of self-preservation. But when we do this we are still moving in the vicious circle of the instincts and have not lifted the soul above its slough. The man who refrains from sin for fear of disease can hardly be said to have escaped from the bondage of sin. His impulse, restrained from manifesting in one form, will soon find an outlet in another. He will not seek to overcome sin, but to make it safe, and he will soon succeed in doing so.

There is only one way to save ourselves from reversion to a lower type when once the undertow of nature sets in, and that is to bring ourselves into touch with a spiritual influence. Let us never forget that there is just as definite an uprush as there is an undertow, and that if we come within the sphere of a spiritual influence, we shall have to use force to resist it, just as much as if we came within the sphere of a debasing influence.

How can we bring spiritual influences to bear on those we wish to help ? By ourselves living the life of the Spirit, in touch with God. Far more potent than words is the invisible force that emanates from the man or woman who is in touch with God.

How can we, if we ourselves are in danger from that dark undertow, bring ourselves into the sphere of spiritual influence ? By putting ourselves into touch with those who themselves are in touch with God, the greatest of whom is Our Lord. If we turn aside for a few moments each day from our obsessing problems to read His life and words, we shall find that we have insensibly been drawn into the sphere of spiritual influence where the current sets Godward.

THE NINETEENTH SUNDAY AFTER TRINITY

" O God, forasmuch as without thee we are not able to please thee ; mercifully grant that thy Holy Spirit may in all things direct and rule our hearts ; through Jesus Christ our Lord. Amen."

KEYNOTE : TAUGHT OF GOD

We are sometimes tempted to resent the fact that without Divine help we cannot rise to the spiritual heights. Perhaps if we had a better understanding of the processes that go on in the soul in the course of its regeneration—if we had some understanding of spiritual psychology—we should be less inclined to dispute what, when all is said and done, is a bare statement of fact, well known to all who have had experience of the Mystic Path.

Let us look at the matter in this way. How could we expect a child, untrained, uneducated, to grow up into a cultured man ? It is well known that children who are cut off from human intercourse, although of normal intelligence, never even develop articulate speech. And so with ourselves, if no higher Light ever shone upon the soul could we, unaided, think out for ourselves the ideal and practice of the spiritual life ?

Mortal man has to acquire ideas totally apart from

those that come to him through the five physical senses if he is to get any realisation of the spiritual life. Without the divine influence from the Divine Mind ever pouring out upon the world, we could form no conception of the nature of God. It is noteworthy that those who try to conceive of God without having had any experience of this Divine Influence have met with little success in their self-imposed task. It is not the faculties of the human mind, its reason and its scholarship, that enables us to understand God, but the inner awareness of the Divine Influence.

To understand God, we must be taught of God, and no other teacher can do more than help us to clarify the impressions thus obtained and arrange our ideas.

THE TWENTIETH SUNDAY AFTER TRINITY

"O ALMIGHTY and most merciful God, keep us, we beseech thee, from all things that may hurt us ; that we, being ready both in body and soul, may cheerfully accomplish those things that thou wouldest have done ; through Jesus Christ our Lord. Amen."

KEYNOTE : ANSWERED PRAYERS

This collect is the prayer of those who dedicate themselves to God's service, and it invokes protection while upon that service.

We often hear people complain that their prayers receive no answer ; and then, on the other hand, we hear examples of wonderful answers to the prayers offered up by men and women dedicated to God. It may be argued that the nature of the prayers do not differ so much, that both may ask for comfort, for strength, for help in their difficulties, but if we observe, we shall notice that the conditions under which the prayers are offered differ greatly. The one man seeks to make use of God, the other seeks to serve God better by obtaining the adjustment of mundane conditions which impair that service.

A King's Messenger, in pursuit of his duties, has a safe conduct through all countries ; but a private individual travelling for his own pleasure has no such privilege, and must make his own arrangements.

If we give our lives to God to be used in His service, even if that service be but the simple duties and obligations of our daily round, done to the glory of God and the service of our brothers, we shall find that our call for help in our daily needs does not pass unanswered, as many can bear witness. If we are struggling with moral problems in our natures—if we are seeking spiritual light when the lamp of our own insight has gone out, we shall find that the invocation of prayer brings immediate results, more than we can ask or think ; but if we ask God to smooth the path of our ambitions or self-indulgence, if we ask Him to remove the consequences of our own lack of forethought or carelessness, we shall find that we are left to learn the lessons of experience. But if, on the contrary, we pray for help in our difficulties in order that we may be ready to serve God the better, we shall find that we have invoked great spiritual forces that work with us to the glory of God.

THE TWENTY-FIRST SUNDAY AFTER TRINITY

" GRANT, we beseech thee, merciful Lord, to thy faithful people pardon and peace, that they may be cleansed from all their sins, and serve thee with a quiet mind; through Jesus Christ our Lord. Amen."

KEYNOTE: FORGIVENESS OF SINS

The more we strive to dedicate our lives to God's service, the more are we conscious of our own imperfections. As our experience of the spiritual life is developed, our sensitiveness to evil increases. Were this to continue indefinitely, we should get into such a morbid condition of scrupulousness that all action would be paralysed, and our end would not be holiness, but insanity.

The Church, therefore, while emphasising the evils of sin, also stresses the power of pardon. The collect for this week contains some very subtle psychology. Firstly, it says that pardon is for the faithful. It is not limited to the righteous who have never erred, nor is it limited to those who have overcome their faults, but is for those who are sincerely doing their best, irrespective of their success.

This may seem an unfair condonation of evil, but let us remember that sin is overcome in the subjective sphere by realisation and regret, by a sincere desire for amendment, and willingness to shoulder the consequences without whining. The clearing-up of the consequences of sin on the physical plane, consequences which may have passed beyond our control, is in a different category from the clearing-up of the causes of sin in the inner consciousness.

Let us, therefore, if we are burdened with a sense of wrong-doing, remember that although we may still have to face the consequences of our acts on the physical plane, we can remove the causes of sin by a change of heart, and when that change of heart takes place, our Father " runs to meet us " and forgives us forthwith.

THE TWENTY-SECOND SUNDAY
AFTER TRINITY

" LORD, we beseech thee to keep thy household the Church in continual godliness ; that through thy protection it may be free from all adversities, and devoutly given to serve thee in good works, to the glory of thy Name ; through Jesus Christ our Lord. Amen."

KEYNOTE : THE HOUSEHOLD OF GOD

The collect speaks of the Church as God's household, and thus puts before us a very beautiful concept of religious life. In thinking of the Church, however, let us not look upon it as one of the many mundane organisations for Christian worship, but rather as that Church on the Spiritual Plane whose head is Christ and whose members are all those who look to Him as Master, Teacher, or Saviour, irrespective of their theology.

Such a family has many members ; each with their own character and viewpoint, each with their duties to the household and their work to do in the outer world, and each entitled to individual freedom of character-development. Such a family of adults cannot be united under a common discipline because of their diversity of individuality, but they can be held together in perfect freedom and yet perfect unity by the bond of love.

This should be our ideal for the " Household of

Christ ; " let its different members realise that they each and all belong to a family of which the Master Jesus is the Head, and that while each does its own work in the world, a common bond unites them.

Let us, for this week, meditate upon the unity of Christendom.

THE TWENTY-THIRD SUNDAY AFTER TRINITY

" O God, our refuge and strength, who art the author of all godliness ; be ready, we beseech thee, to hear the devout prayers of thy Church ; and grant that those things which we ask faithfully we may obtain effectually ; through Jesus Christ our Lord. Amen."

KEYNOTE : PRAYERS THAT ARE ANSWERED

Those things for which we ask faithfully we shall obtain effectually. We need have no doubt of that. But what does it mean to ask faithfully ? There are several different senses of this word given in the dictionary, and according to our choice of a meaning will be our understanding of the requisite conditions of effectual prayer.

Is faith synonymous with belief ? If this be the case, it is only necessary to believe blindly in order to pray effectually ; but experience proves otherwise. Blind belief often meets with disappointment, or has to be content to rationalise what an unprejudiced observer would consider to be failure.

But there are other meanings to the word " faithful," and among them are " loyal," " true to fact," " accurate." Has it ever occurred to you that it is necessary that we should pray " accurately " if we are to obtain

results ? That the spirit of our prayers must be " loyal "
to the law of God ?   " Not my will, but Thine be done,"
said Our Lord in His supreme prayer in the Garden of
Gethsemane.

When, seeking to fulfil God's law we invoke God's
help, we shall be heard of our Father. Strength, understanding, and peace flow into our hearts when this, the
only true prayer, goes up to God, and our Heavenly
Father grants our petition, not by a miracle to astonish
the crowd, but by something far better than a miracle,
the coming into operation of the laws whereby He
" sweetly and rightly ordereth all things " and which
only await our fulfilment of the conditions of their
operation to become effectual in our lives.

THE TWENTY-FOURTH SUNDAY
AFTER TRINITY

" O LORD, we beseech thee, absolve thy people from their offences ; that through thy bountiful goodness we may all be delivered from the bands of those sins, which by our frailty we have committed ; grant this, O heavenly Father, for Jesus Christ's sake, our blessed Lord and Saviour. Amen."

KEYNOTE : ABSOLUTION

The concept of absolution contains more than the concept of the forgiveness of sins. Our sins may be forgiven, our moral guilt may be ended, and yet we may have to endure the consequences of our wrong-doing. But absolution implies the remission of the penalty as well as the pardoning of the transgression. How are we to harmonise this concept with that of universal law, and of action and reaction as unvaryingly equal and opposite ?

Implicit in the Christian religion, and in the Christian religion only, is the doctrine of the forgiveness of sins so complete that even the inevitable reaction does not take place. This doctrine is the logical outcome of the doctrine of Sacrifice if that great natural truth be rightly understood.

What is sacrifice ? It is not the destruction of the

thing sacrificed, for nothing that exists can be destroyed, it can only be transmuted. That which is burnt does not cease to exist, it is reduced to so much carbon, mineral salts, and water. When we make the complete sacrifice of the self which is implicit in the word surrender, the forces of our nature that were previously used for selfish, even if not for actually evil ends, are transmuted into a higher type of force, and it is this force which neutralises upon the Inner Planes the forces which our sin set in motion. It is only when the redemption of the whole nature takes place that we are freed from the consequences of our sin. We are freed because we have worked out the problem on the Inner planes, and we are able to do this because Our Lord Jesus Christ showed us the way—the Way of the Cross, which is sacrifice's supreme symbol.

THE TWENTY-FIFTH SUNDAY AFTER TRINITY

" Stir up, we beseech thee, the wills of thy faithful people ; that they, plenteously bringing forth the fruit of good works, may of thee be plenteously rewarded ; through Jesus Christ our Lord. Amen."

KEYNOTE : THE WORK OF THE WILL

God's grace is a spiritual potency which works on the spiritual side of our nature ; but for its powers to be brought through into manifestation in our lives, to work regeneratively in our characters and circumstances, each level in our nature must co-operate and play its part, performing the especial work in the polity of humanity which falls to its lot.

To invoke God's grace and leave it at that leads to the certainty of disappointment. Our reasoning faculties must think things out and arrive at a just assessment of the facts ; and finally, but most vitally, the will must bring all our energies to a focus and direct them to a single point. When this is done we shall find that these three factors, God's grace, an honest judgment, and a concentrated will are equal to any problems that life can set them.

It is this concentrated, energised will which is of such importance in the spiritual life. God has as little use for backboneless worshippers as has Mammon. But what is this difficulty over the weakness of our wills which so often besets us ? So many people complain that the good they would, they do not ; and the evil they would not, that they do. Perhaps if we understood the psychology of the will better, we should obtain a little more insight into their problem.

The will is not a factor in itself, it is simply the focusing of the forces of our nature. If we are able readily to bring all our forces to a single focus, directed to a single object, and maintain that concentration steadily over a period of time, we are said to have strong wills. The weak will is not caused by any lack of the faculty for willing, but by the diffusion of our interest and desires over many objects instead of their concentration upon one.

We can see this very clearly in the case of the drunkard, who is said to be so weak-willed that he cannot perform any consecutive work nor abstain from alcohol, yet who, when it comes to obtaining alcohol, will show the utmost concentration of energy, pertinacity, and will-power.

It is not that we are weak-willed, as that we are diffuse of desires. If we are going to achieve anything, we must be prepared to sacrifice something, to prune away the redundant things in our lives, and make even our legitimate needs queue up and take their turn. Nothing can be achieved in any walk of life without sacrifice, and the spiritual life is far from being an exception to this rule. Strength of will has its roots in a capacity for sacrifice— that is the real secret of its nature.

If we want a thing sufficiently badly, we will make any sacrifice to obtain it. The man who bought the pearl of great price had a strong will.

SAINT ANDREW'S DAY

" ALMIGHTY God, who didst give such grace unto thy holy Apostle Saint Andrew, that he readily obeyed the calling of thy Son Jesus Christ, and followed him without delay ; grant unto us all, that we, being called by thy holy Word, may forthwith give up ourselves obediently to fulfil thy holy commandments ; through the same Jesus Christ our Lord. Amen."

KEYNOTE : ANSWERING THE CALL

When Our Lord, walking by the Sea of Galilee, called Andrew and Peter his brother to be His disciples, we are told that " straightway they left their nets and followed Him."

This immediate and complete response to the call of Our Lord is recorded of others beside these two brothers, fishermen of the Sea of Galilee. James and John likewise, and Saint Paul, after his conversion, left all and followed Him. In the lives of the saints we also see this sudden and complete turning to God in many cases, though in others there may be a prolonged and painful struggle before the final surrender takes place.

Our Lord in many parables points out this same fact—that we can only enter into the Kingdom by passing through the gate that is straight.

It is for this reason that so many who seek Our Lord

quite sincerely, fail to find Him. They hear His call, and say " Wait, Lord, till I haul in my net." When they reach the bank, there is no one there. Andrew and his brother did not do that. They left their nets and followed Him, and therefore they found Him. Their nets might drift with the tide, but they needed them no longer, for they had become fishers of men.

None who serve Our Lord are without their reward, but it is only those who give their whole selves to Him who are able to show the " signs following."

It is the complete change of standpoint which is necessary when we enter upon the spiritual life. We can only hope to achieve in the life of the world by hard work, concentration, and singleness of purpose ; so it is with the Mystic Way ; the spiritual dilettante has as little hope of reaching the heights of his faith as has the dabbler in other walks of life. There are too many amateur Christians who go in for religion in their spare time.

What God needs are men and women who, when they realise the truth, change all their values and the standpoint from which they view life, and unhesitatingly " cut their losses."   When they do this, the laws of the spiritual plane come into action for them and all their needs are supplied, for they can say with Our Lord, " I have bread to eat ye know not of."

It is the nerveless follower of Our Lord, who has let go his grip on the world and failed to lay hold of the Kingdom, who falls by the way.

SAINT THOMAS THE APOSTLE

" ALMIGHTY and everliving God, who for the more confirmation of the faith didst suffer thy holy Apostle Thomas to be doubtful in thy Son's resurrection ; grant us so perfectly and without all doubt, to believe in thy Son Jesus Christ, that our faith in thy sight may never be reproved. Hear us, O Lord, through the same Jesus Christ, to whom, with thee and the Holy Ghost, be all honour and glory, now and for evermore. Amen."

KEYNOTE : FAITH

Faith is a thing which cannot be forced ; it wells up from the depths of the soul spontaneously. It is not the same thing as belief or knowledge. We believe a thing because the evidence is strong in its favour. We know a thing as the result of first-hand experience. Faith differs from belief in that we cannot receive it at second-hand ; it differs from knowledge in that it has no tangible grounds. What then is faith ? Is there a third type of consciousness to which it corresponds ?

Yes, there is, says the New Psychology ; it corresponds to subconsciousness, and we can define faith as the conscious result of subconscious experience. That is to say, the soul has had experiences which the brain is unable to cognise because they have taken place below the threshold of consciousness. Nevertheless, we feel their effects, even as we feel the effects of a subconscious pathology. A dissociated memory can change the whole nature of a man from normal to abnormal ; even so a mystical experience, which is never brought through to consciousness, can change his whole attitude towards life, and give him a realisation and conviction that no arguments, however logical, could ever produce.

Faith, the fruit of subconscious spiritual experience, is the precursor of conscious spiritual experience. The science which deals with the two is called mystical theology. We might more aptly call it mystical psychology, for it deals not so much with the nature of God as with the processes of consciousness whereby man apprehends God.

How are we, who walk in darkness, to see this great Light ? Arguments based on psychology may give us the certainty that our quest is not in vain, even as arguments based on geometry gave Columbus his certainty of finding land across the Atlantic. How are we to navigate the shoreless ocean of inner experience and make the landfall of the Kingdom ? We need to develop a new type of consciousness, a new method of using the mind. Perhaps we can learn something from watching the man who wants to start the engine of his car. What does he do ? He turns it over by hand repeatedly, till finally a spark is generated, the petrol vapour is fired, and the engine takes up its work.

That is exactly what we have to do when we are endeavouring to acquire faith—we have to turn our spiritual life over by hand until a spark of Divine Power is generated in it. We have to live our inner life " as if " we had faith ; we have to do, by an act of will, the things the believer does, pray as he prays, worship as he worships,

taking our religion as a working hypothesis. If we do
this sufficiently pertinaciously (and an engine takes a lot
of starting on a cold morning), there comes a time when
a spark will reward our effort and the power of the Holy
Ghost will be upon us.

THE CONVERSION OF SAINT PAUL

" O God, who, through the preaching of the blessed Apostle Saint Paul, hast caused the light of the Gospel to shine throughout the world ; grant, we beseech thee, that we, having his wonderful conversion in remembrance, may show forth our thankfulness unto thee for the same, by following the holy doctrine which he taught ; through Jesus Christ our Lord.   Amen."

KEYNOTE : THE REALITY OF SPIRITUAL THINGS

The conversion of Saint Paul is one of those things which arrest the attention of even the most indifferent. It was too well-attested, it was too generally accepted by his contemporaries, for the facts to be in dispute.   The only matter for debate is the interpretation to be placed on these facts.

And what are the actual facts ?   Briefly, Saul of Tarsus, while travelling to Damascus in order to take drastic action against certain heretics, had a seizure which left him blind for several days.   Then his sight returned as suddenly as it had gone, and from being a strictly orthodox Jew and persecutor of the Christians, he became one of their most ardent supporters.

In what does this sudden illness of the Jewish traveller differ from an ordinary attack of epilepsy, to which, at

first sight, it bears a close resemblance ? It differs in
this, that the result was a complete change of life, of
character, and of consciousness. It is obvious that the
real focus of the event was in the mind and not in the
body, and that what happened to the physical form of
the Jew upon that Syrian road was but the repercussion
of what took place in his consciousness. The power
that descended upon him spent its force on his soul,
and his body only got the aftermath. That is obvious to
anyone who looks candidly at the facts, and does not
seek to explain them away by a hypothesis that shall
reconcile them with preconceived ideas.

There are many things in the spiritual life which
cannot be explained in this fashion. We have no terms
derived from sensory experience in which to express
them ; they can only be described in terms of spiritual
experience, and those who have not had any opening of
the higher consciousness will make nothing of such
explanations. Those, however, who have had even the
first foreshadowing of a mystical experience will understand, because they know that a whole new world of
experience is opened up by the development of the
higher consciousness and the plane of things it contacts.

Such happenings as the conversion of Saint Paul force
upon us the realisation that the horizon of our senses
does not mark the circle of eternity. There are things
of which we are unaware because normally we have no
senses to perceive them ; nevertheless, they are among
the most vital potencies of the universe.

It is these things that the mystics touch with their
extended consciousness. It is here that the validities of
religion are found. It is out of such experiences as these
that men have built up religion ; and if we were able to
share in them, we should be aware of the reality behind

religion, and know that it is not a concerted fraud that pious men have forced on humanity for generations.

It is this reality behind religion that we need to seek, not resting content with the formal performance of religious duties, but rather, with eager expectation striving for the illumination that dawns upon the soul that has found God and causes its whole life to light up and shine forth as a beacon to other wanderers in the darkness of sense-limitation.

THE PRESENTATION OF CHRIST IN THE TEMPLE

" ALMIGHTY and everliving God, we humbly beseech thy Majesty, that, as thy only-begotten Son was this day presented in the temple in substance of our flesh, so we may be presented unto thee with pure and clean hearts, by the same thy Son Jesus Christ our Lord. Amen."

KEYNOTE : PERCEPTION OF SPIRITUAL TRUTH

The attitude of the priests of the great temple at Jerusalem towards Our Lord is a thing which must give us food for thought, especially if we are of those who might be numbered among the doctors of Israel.

It was not the high priest of Israel who announced that the Dayspring from on high had come, but an obscure man and an aged woman of the people who recognised the Child-Christ in His infancy, and declared that the Sun of Righteousness was above the horizon of human consciousness.

We all need constantly to review our attitude towards Truth. We can never hope to know it in its entirety, and for this very reason we should always keep open the door of the mind. By how many parables and teachings did our Master emphasise the fact that Truth comes when it is least expected and from places where we should never look for it. It is only by keeping our souls sensitive to its influence that we can hope to recognise it when it thus suddenly comes upon us in some humble guise.

Humility is the key of that door in the soul that opens to the Christ. The priest, proud in his established position, took the unknown Child in his arms and blessed Him perfunctorily. The influence radiating from the Divine Child did not cause his heart to burn within him. How often may we, who believe that we have some degree of knowledge and experience, pass by the Christ-teaching unnoticed ?

Unless we are constantly on the alert to all that is noble and beautiful and sincere and pure, we are in danger of overlooking the Christ. We must get away from the spiritual snobbery that cannot see profundity in any teaching unless it has the hall-mark of authority. The wind of the Spirit bloweth where it listeth ; the light of the Spirit shines out from those whose hearts are near to God. In whatever form the Christ comes to us, whether it be as a little Child in poor swaddling-clothes, or as the King of Glory, let us open to Him the door.

SAINT MATTHIAS'S DAY

" O ALMIGHTY God, who into the place of the traitor Judas didst choose thy faithful servant Matthias to be of the number of the twelve Apostles ; grant that thy Church, being alway preserved from false Apostles, may be ordered and guided by faithful and true pastors ; through Jesus Christ our Lord. Amen."

KEYNOTE : SPIRITUAL FUNCTIONING

Saint Matthias was elected by his brethren to fill the vacancy created by the suicide of Judas Iscariot. What lesson can this fact teach us ? What guidance can it offer us in the pursuit of the spiritual life ?

We see that Judas was not able to retain his position as one of the Twelve after his spiritual consciousness was darkened, for he held his place, not by any legal right, but by function.

This is the great lesson which the election of Saint Matthias has for the Church. She can only hope to be the Church of Christ for just as long as she manifests the power of the Christ. When that departs, the glory is departed. Ichabod will be written on her walls, and the power will reappear wherever the illuminated spiritual consciousness shall open a channel.

No man can command the Spirit of God. It bloweth where it listeth. It is no respecter of persons, but manifests where it can find a channel.

Organisations are convenient, but they are not essential. Nothing is essential to the spiritual life save the spirit of God. When that breath passes from the body corporate of the Church, She will die. As long as it remains, no human hand can deal Her a death-blow.

Whatever organisation opens a channel for God's power will be filled with that power, even as water seeks its own level. The Church holds her pre-eminence by being the broadest and deepest channel, the most universal expression of man's spiritual aspirations, that at the moment we possess.

But should that channel become choked, should a deeper and straighter channel be opened, the power will flow therein, and none can stay it.

And why should we seek to stay it ? What does it matter who feeds the sheep so long as they are fed ? What does it matter who does God's work so long as His work gets done ? Well for us if our hands be found worthy ; but the main thing is that the work should be done, not that our prestige should be maintained.

A church is a church and a priest is a priest when spiritual function is present. When it is absent, no laying on of hands, no claims to Apostolic Succession, even if confirmed by Act of Parliament, are going to maintain the dead in life.

Function is all the Church needs to maintain her rights. Let her function, and none can gainsay her.

THE ANNUNCIATION OF THE BLESSED VIRGIN MARY

" WE beseech thee, O Lord, pour thy grace into our hearts ; that, as we have known the incarnation of thy Son Jesus Christ by the message of an angel, so by his cross and passion we may be brought unto the glory of his resurrection ; through the same Jesus Christ our Lord. Amen."

KEYNOTE : SELF-PREPARATION

Can we not picture the bewilderment of Mary of the hill-town of Nazareth when the angel of the Lord announced unto her her destiny ?

How many of us, were we called to do a great work for God, could rise to the occasion ? And what would be our regrets, after the angelic Messenger had turned away sorrowful, that we were not found ready, with our loins girt and our lamps burning.

The spiritual life is a great adventure. We never know what may come to us out of the Unseen. What tests, what triumphs. Let us therefore always have our lamps trimmed and our staffs ready to hand, lest the great opportunity come and we miss it.

We should aim each day so to live, so to keep our higher consciousness open, that should the call come to us to rise up and serve God, we shall not be found wanting. We should take all human steps towards that end ; we should make all human preparations that are possible to us.

In small things we should train ourselves day by day ; we should learn courage, selflessness, purity, singleness of purpose, fidelity—from the experiences of our daily life ; if we cannot learn them thus, there is no other school open to us.

Let us think of Our Lady, living quietly in her father's house in Nazareth, fulfilling all the daily tasks of her home, to whom the Angel came so suddenly, un-heralded. If that day there had been confusion and dispute, ill-will or complaining, would she have been in any frame of mind to receive her angelic visitant ?

How many times may the Messenger of God have turned away from our door without knocking because he heard the sound of angry voices within ?

From this day onwards, let us always be mindful, when we raise our voices, of Who may be standing on the threshold, about to knock.

SAINT MARK'S DAY

" O Almighty God, who hast instructed thy holy
Church with the heavenly doctrine of thy Evangelist
Saint Mark ; give us grace, that, being not like children
carried away with every blast of vain doctrine, we may
be established in the truth of thy holy Gospel ; through
Jesus Christ our Lord. Amen."

KEYNOTE : DISCERNMENT OF THE TRUTH

In spiritual matters it is very easy to be deceived, for
they are inner experiences, they are matters of feeling
and states of consciousness, and it is not possible to
subject them to the tests which we can apply to material
happenings.

It is, therefore, essential to us that we should have
some standard to which they correspond by which to
judge them. How and where are we to find such an
external standard in these matters of inner experience,
which we can in no way externalise save by the expression
of them in a language which is not designed for such
uses ?

If, day by day, we return constantly to the record of
Our Lord's earthly life, so that the atmosphere of His
influence ever pervades our consciousness, we shall
intuitively react to all that comes our way, and we shall
know by our reactions whether it be of God or no.

Just as the ear of the musician can be trained to a subtle discrimination of tones, so can the soul of the lover of God be trained to a subtle discrimination of truth. If we be imbued with the Christ-spirit, whatever is inimical to that spirit will strike a false note in our ears, and we shall need no doctrinal learning to show us its falsity, we shall *hear* with the ears of the spirit.

The musician does not need to argue from the theory of harmony to prove that a note is false ; he hears its discordant vibrations, and that is enough for him. But he cannot discriminate between the false and the true unless he has the true ever ringing in his ears. And so he always carries a tuning-fork or pitch-pipe with him, and when in doubt he strikes a note of absolutely pure tone, and instantly his ear tells him whether the instrument he hears is in tune or not.

For us, the Gospels are our pitch-pipe. Let us always have them with us, and if we are in doubt concerning any spiritual matter, let us read in them, and then, having thus tuned our minds, reconsider the problem, and we shall hear at once if it strikes an un-Christlike note.

SAINT PHILIP AND SAINT JAMES'S DAY

" O ALMIGHTY God, whom truly to know is everlasting life ; grant us perfectly to know thy Son Jesus Christ to be the way, the truth, and the life ; that, following the steps of thy holy Apostles, Saint Philip and Saint James, we may stedfastly walk in the way that leadeth to eternal life ; through the same thy Son Jesus Christ our Lord. Amen."

KEYNOTE : KNOWLEDGE OF THE WAY

" Whither I go, ye know, and the way ye know," said Our Lord. In His Personality He showed us the Father by manifesting the Divine qualities ; in His life He showed us the Way by treading it Himself. Not otherwise could man ever have learned anything concerning the nature of God, for the things of the Kingdom transcend human apprehension, not being of this world, and we can only perceive them when they are translated into terms of human life.

The Divine Life is expressed in the divine qualities of the human spirit. Those characteristics which we recognise as Christlike " show us the Father." To preach Christ Crucified is useless unless we ourselves know what it means to bear one another's burdens. We have to *show* people the Father, not tell them about Him. The surest way to win souls for God is to try to lead the Christ-life ourselves and let its beauty attract them.

All that we can ever know of God on this earth is that beam of His radiance which is able to shine through the lens of human living. The Kingdom of Heaven on earth is made with hands. It is not enough to pray, " Thy kingdom come." We must go and fetch it.

SAINT BARNABAS THE APOSTLE

" O LORD God Almighty, who didst endue thy holy
Apostle Barnabas with singular gifts of the Holy Ghost ;
leave us not, we beseech thee, destitute of thy manifold
gifts, nor yet of grace to use them alway to thy honour
and glory ; through Jesus Christ our Lord. Amen."

KEYNOTE : GOODNESS

There is no gift we can bring to the altar of dedication
that is more acceptable unto God than simple goodness
of life. There is no other basis on which Christ's
Church can be built, for it is the one thing that stands
firm amid shifting sands of time and fate.

Intellectual gifts, whether of profundity or brilliancy,
will prove destructive to their possessor unless there be
that underlying stability of goodness.

Mystical vision, unless it be securely bedded in goodness of life, will end in illusion. Even the dedicated life
of self-denial and adoration will not prove acceptable
unto God unless simple human goodness be its basis.

This is the rock on which all things are built, for it is
the only source of security, and without security the
loftiest attainments are worthless. The higher we climb,
the greater our fall.

Out of an abiding sense of fairness, of duty, of truth,
and of kindliness the kingdom of heaven is wrought upon
earth.

SAINT JOHN BAPTIST'S DAY

"ALMIGHTY God, by whose providence thy servant John Baptist was wonderfully born, and sent to prepare the way of thy Son our Saviour, by preaching of repentance ; make us so to follow his doctrine and holy life, that we may truly repent according to his preaching ; and after his example constantly speak the truth, boldly rebuke vice, and patiently suffer for the truth's sake ; through Jesus Christ our Lord. Amen."

KEYNOTE : STRAIGHTNESS

Before Israel saw her Saviour she heard the voice of one crying in the wilderness, " Repent, for the kingdom of heaven is at hand. Prepare ye the way of the Lord. Make His paths straight."

When we seek to find Our Lord, praying for His grace to come to us, for His peace to be upon us, for the illumination of His presence to be all about us, do we always remember that the coming of John the Baptist preceded the Coming of our Blessed Lord ?

We must perform the human part of the task before we can ask Our Lord to perform the divine part. We must be honest and true and doing our best before we ask for God's grace to help us to do better.

The Power of the Lord will surely come upon us in response to our supplication, but we must make straight its paths through our soul. There must be no tortuousness in our nature if the great spiritual forces are to work through us.

The noble quality of " straightness " is essential to the Christian character. It was those who lacked " straightness " whom Our Lord called " whited sepulchres."

There is nothing that more surely brings Our Lord's name into contempt among men and estranges them from Him than the spectacle of one who follows in His footsteps and yet lacks the fundamental quality of Straightness. There is nothing, no gift of tongues, no liberality of charity, no selflessness or sacrifice which will offset the lack of this fundamental quality.

It is lack of courage which is responsible for this failure. Men go by devious ways because they fear the consequences of going straight. If we realised, however, that all is governed by the absolute law of God, which swerves not a hair's breadth, we should fear much more to go crooked than to go straight, knowing the inevitableness of the day of reckoning. We should resolutely cut our losses until we found our feet on firm ground.

It was the moral courage of John the Baptist which was his greatest characteristic ; and it was shown not only in his rebuke of Herod, but also in his acknowledgment of Jesus. What must it have meant to a man already famous and with a large following, to say, " There is one that comes after me, the latchet of whose shoes I am not worthy to unloosen. He must grow greater, and I must grow less," and to ask for a blessing from the unknown Stranger who came to him demanding baptism !

It was this moral courage of John the Baptist's which

enabled him to discern the Christ. It was the time-serving of the priests which prevented them from recognising Him.

One who has given all to God has nothing to fear because he has nothing to lose. All is Christ's and He can take care of His own.

SAINT PETER'S DAY

" O ALMIGHTY God, who by thy Son Jesus Christ didst give to thy Apostle Saint Peter many excellent gifts, and commandedst him earnestly to feed thy flock; make, we beseech thee, all Bishops and Pastors diligently to preach thy holy Word, and the people obediently to follow the same, that they may receive the crown of everlasting glory; through Jesus Christ our Lord. Amen."

KEYNOTE: MORAL COURAGE

Saint Peter was characterised by two things—the heights to which he could rise, and the depths to which he could fall. It was he who discerned that Jesus was the Son of God, and it was he also who denied Him. But through all, he maintained an absolute sincerity, an absolute spiritual honesty. After he had denied his Lord he went out and wept bitterly, but he ceased not from following Him. After such a failure it must have required great moral courage to take up his cross once more and follow the Christ. It must have required equally great courage to face the other disciples again, admitting his failure. Yet Saint Peter did it.

Herein is a great lesson for us. However often we may deny Our Lord, He never denies us. The way is always open for us to turn again and " make good " even as the great apostle did, provided that like him, we do not try to justify our weaknesses.

Paradoxical as it may seem in one who denied his Master, it is moral courage that is the keynote of Saint Peter's life. He it is who, being the corner-stone of the Church, is the especial patron of all priests and bishops and servants of God wherever they are found. They, more than all others, are in need of his cardinal quality, for it is no easy thing to stand up in the Name of God in the full light of publicity where every human failing is revealed.

No one is immune from failings, but the great thing is to serve God in spite of them. This is Saint Peter's lesson to us, that we should stand up in that highest courage, that truest humility, which is not afraid of its own past but goes on in spite of it, enduring the scorn of men and leaving the issue in God's hands ; which bows its head to the storm and trudges steadily onwards in the footsteps of the Master.

SAINT JAMES THE APOSTLE

" GRANT, O merciful God, that as thine holy Apostle Saint James, leaving his father and all that he had, without delay was obedient unto the calling of thy Son Jesus Christ, and followed him ; so we, forsaking all worldly and carnal affections, may be evermore ready to follow thy holy commandments ; through Jesus Christ our Lord. Amen."

KEYNOTE : RENUNCIATION

It was Saint James who, immediately Our Lord called, left all and followed Him, and who declared himself ready to drink of the Cup Our Lord drank of, and be baptised with the baptism He was baptised with, and who fulfilled his word, dying by the sword in Jerusalem for the foundation of the Christian Church.

His lesson for us lies in the fact that immediately the call came he took up his Cross and followed his Lord. Once he had realised the nature of the Christ, there was no more questioning ; he left all and followed Him. The Gospel record makes it clear that this was no blind and impulsive following without counting the cost. He was prepared to share in Our Lord's Cup, he followed His footsteps through Galilee till the end, and then died for the faith.

Of those who complain of the barrenness of the

spiritual life, how many are there who would have done what Saint James did ? Or, standing by their nets, did they watch the figure of Our Lord fading away in the distance ? It is not possible to drink the wine of the spirit save out of the Cup of Our Lord.

These are the things we forget when we become fireside followers of His footsteps. The Way of the Cross is a great adventure. The pearls of the inner life only come to those who sell all that they have. Not everyone is ready for the path to the heights, but we should not complain of the lack of spiritual vitality in religion under such circumstances. Unless we do what the saints have done, we must not expect to know God as they knew Him.

The life in religion is our own life, poured out in sacrifice.

SAINT BARTHOLOMEW THE APOSTLE

" O ALMIGHTY and everlasting God, who didst give to thine Apostle Bartholomew grace truly to believe and to preach thy Word ; grant, we beseech thee, unto thy Church, to love that Word which he believed, and both to preach and receive the same ; through Jesus Christ our Lord. Amen."

KEYNOTE : FIDELITY

Saint Bartholomew was never one of the outstanding figures among the disciples. The Bible tells us nothing about him save his name, yet he is always mentioned as being among those who were with Our Lord in all His temptations and he was one of those who were present in the upper chamber when the power of the Holy Spirit came upon the apostles.

Saint Bartholomew teaches us that those who serve faithfully in humble tasks shall in no wise lack their reward. It is not the magnitude of the thing done by which Our Lord judges us. Some may do great things because great opportunities come to them, or because great resources are at their disposal. These have the applause of the world, and they deserve it. But God also reads hearts, and knows that just the same qualities are needed for the faithful performance of humble tasks which never show when they are faithfully done, but would soon be missed if they were left un-done.

God rewards us, not according to the thing done, but according to the qualities of the spirit that went to the doing of it.   Saint Bartholomew, though not one of his sayings and doings were reckoned worthy of record in the Gospels, was nevertheless found worthy to be in the upper chamber when the Holy Spirit came down in tongues of fire.

SAINT MATTHEW THE APOSTLE

" O ALMIGHTY God, who by thy blessed Son didst call Matthew from the receipt of custom to be an Apostle and Evangelist ; grant us grace to forsake all covetous desires, and inordinate love of riches, and to follow the same thy Son Jesus Christ, who liveth and reigneth with thee and the Holy Ghost, one God, world without end. Amen."

KEYNOTE : REGENERATION

When Our Lord called Saint Matthew, he was sitting at the receipt of custom, that is to say, he was a tax-gatherer, collecting the dues of Cæsar, the overlord of Israel ; and as such, representing the oppressor, he was especially an object of hatred and contempt to his fellow-Jews, for he was one who had sold his birthright for a mess of pottage.

Nevertheless, Our Lord discerning the spiritual quality in the soul of Matthew the publican, saw that he had the capacity to respond to the call of the higher life when it came to him.

Jesus never cared what people had been, nor even what they were when He met them ; He only cared for their spiritual possibilities, and addressed His words to the higher self hidden from human eyes but visible to His sympathy and insight. It was this higher self that answered His call in the Magdalen and the tax-gatherer. Let this be a lesson to us never to confuse the personality of a man with his real self. If we see only the lower selves of men, which alone are visible to outward view, we shall not judge truly of their natures ; but if, as did Our Lord, we see also the divine spark of pure spirit at the heart of each living soul, if we remember that by its very nature that spark must fly upwards, then, if we have wisdom and faith, we may be able to call that soul to Christ.

But if we see only the sinner in his wickedness, we shall bind about his neck burdens grievous to be borne ; we shall reinforce the weight of sin already pressing upon him by the weight of our condemnation. Gesture and tone will betray our thought, and the riper that soul is for its healing, the more will it shrink from us. Only the hardened sinner can stand up to condemnation ; the repentant sinner is the sensitive sinner. Let us always take sides with a man's higher self in its struggle with his lower self, and never, even in thought, identify him with his sin.

SAINT MICHAEL AND ALL ANGELS

" O EVERLASTING God, who hast ordained and constituted the services of Angels and men in a wonderful order ; mercifully grant, that as thy holy Angels always do thee service in heaven, so by thy appointment they may succour and defend us on earth ; through Jesus Christ our Lord. Amen."

KEYNOTE : THE INVISIBLE WORLD

In our present materialistic age we deny and ignore many things that were known to the companions of Our Lord and of the prophets before Him, who knew and relied upon the ministry of angels. What are these angelic beings who relieved the necessities of Our Lord after His temptation in the wilderness, who warned God's servants of impending danger, and released apostles from prison ?

May it not be that there are states of existence about which our five physical senses tell us nothing, and that, as the Bible implies, there are indeed organised and intelligent forces of both good and evil which we cannot perceive, yet which nevertheless influence us profoundly ?

We shall never understand the mystery of the world unless we recognise this unseen side of existence. It is the clue to a very great deal that baffles us. The angels of His presence dwell there, also the devils of the evil imaginings of men's hearts. It is upon this, the mind-side of things, that we must seek for the realities and potencies that underlie our world of appearances.

SAINT LUKE THE EVANGELIST

"ALMIGHTY God, who calledst Luke the Physician, whose praise is in the Gospel, to be an Evangelist, and Physician of the soul ; may it please thee, that, by the wholesome medicines of the doctrine delivered by him, all the diseases of our souls may be healed ; through the merits of thy Son Jesus Christ our Lord. Amen."

KEYNOTE : HEALING

Saint Luke was the physician whom Our Lord called from the healing of bodies to heal the soul as well. None knew better than he that the two go together, and that the true healing is not the repair of any part, but the harmonisation of the whole. There is a hygiene of the soul which, if disregarded, will poison the body.

All healing should be spiritual healing, even if its outward form be that of a surgical operation. Every curative process, whether applied to the body in a hospital or the soul in a prison, should be inspired by a spiritual ideal.

The curative art means a readjustment. There is but one absolute standard by which anything can be re-adjusted, and that is natural law, or the nature of God. All healing therefore, whether of mind, body, or estate, must aim at bringing that which is amiss into harmony with God's law, that is to say, God's nature as shown us by His Son.

The Great Physician is the Master of all who would make straight that which is crooked, provided they do it for the glory of God and the service of man, and not to their own aggrandisement. His spirit it is which should illuminate all healing work and overshadow every hospital and prison, for in His spirit alone can they fulfil their mission.

SAINT SIMON AND SAINT JUDE, APOSTLES

" O ALMIGHTY God, who hast built thy Church upon the foundation of the Apostles and Prophets, Jesus Christ himself being the head corner-stone ; grant us so to be joined together in unity of spirit by their doctrine, that we may be made an holy temple acceptable unto thee ; through Jesus Christ our Lord. Amen."

KEYNOTE : HUMILITY

It is well for us to remember those of Our Lord's companions who stood in the background, and not merely concentrate our attention upon those great figures of the Gospel story who stand out in the forefront of the record.

Hebrew names always have a meaning, and when we come to interpret those of Saint Simon and Saint Jude we find they mean the One who Hears and the One who Praises. So we can imagine these two quiet figures, hearing and praising Our Lord, and seeking not their own.

It was not until the end of their lives that His disciples were called upon to die for the Master ; but day by day along the hot Syrian roads they were called upon to live for Him, and the greatest service they could do Him, the most powerful support they could give Him in His work, was to keep unbroken the bond of brotherhood among themselves, for how could He commune with His Father if the sound of bickering were in His ears ?

These humble souls, who companioned Him so faithfully and who were loyal to each other through all difficulties and good and ill report, are brethren to all those who bear the world's burdens unnoticed. They are the patron saints of the rank and file. Their quiet, workaday virtues it was that helped to hold together the band of disciples when Peter blew hot and cold and John was wrapt away in vision.

And so it is with us. These humble virtues are the basis of all stability, and having them, we shall in no wise lack our reward when Our Master calls upon those who have been faithful over the few things to bear rule over many.

ALL SAINTS' DAY

" O Almighty God, who hast knit together thine elect
in one communion and fellowship, in the mystical body
of thy Son Christ our Lord ; grant us grace so to follow
thy blessed Saints in all virtuous and godly living, that
we may come to those unspeakable joys, which thou
hast prepared for them that unfeignedly love thee ;
through Jesus Christ our Lord. Amen."

KEYNOTE : THE COMRADESHIP OF THE PATH

There have gone before us by the Way of the Cross an
innumerable company of men and women ; and we, if
we too be following the Master, are of their fellowship.

This comradeship upon the Path is very precious to
us in the Christian communion, for it gives us assurance
that our efforts are not in vain, for others have won to
the heights towards which we are striving. We have
dreamed no idle dream, for upon the summit we can see
the figures of those who have gone before us.

As they have achieved, even so can we achieve *if we
are prepared to pay the price that they paid*. And even
if that be beyond our spiritual means, nevertheless, if we
give but a cup of cold water to Christ's little ones, we
shall in no wise lack our reward. All who tread in His
footsteps are on the Path, and are comrades.

There is nothing that can befall us upon the Path which they have not known before us. Its stones and its steep places are all known to them. When we are in doubt as to the way, or are mindful to turn back, let us take counsel with them and see how they met and overcame the problems that are besetting us. What one has done, another can do. We have no excuse for turning back if we can see imprinted upon the Path the footsteps of those who have gone before. Where they have gone, we can go, if we have the courage, for the source of their strength is available for us also ; and at the end of the journey, Christ awaits us, to say, " Well done, thou good and faithful servant, enter thou into the joy of thy Lord."